THANK GOD FOR CANCER
MY TRANSFORMATION JOURNEY

Joann Brown

Author's Tranquility Press
MARIETTA, GEORGIA

Copyright © 2021 by Joann Brown.

All rights reserved. No part of this publication may be reproduced, distributed or transmitted in any form or by any means, including photocopying, recording, or other electronic or mechanical methods, without the prior written permission of the publisher, except in the case of brief quotations embodied in critical reviews and certain other noncommercial uses permitted by copyright law. For permission requests, write to the publisher, addressed "Attention: Permissions Coordinator," at the address below.

Joann Brown /Author's Tranquility Press
2706 Station Club Drive SW
Marietta, GA 30060
www.authorstranquilitypress.com

Publisher's Note: This is a work of non-fiction. Names, characters, places, and incidents have been changed to protect the people behind the story.

Ordering Information:
Quantity sales. Special discounts are available on quantity purchases by corporations, associations, and others. For details, contact the "Special Sales Department" at the address above.

Thank God for Cancer/ Joann Brown
Paperback: 978-1-956480-14-6
eBook: 978-1-956480-15-3

DEDICATION

*This book is dedicated in honor of my first daughter-in-law, Lena White, and to all of the other sisters of breast cancer that are now **resting healed** from all of this world's sicknesses, troubles, and pains in **JESUS CHRIST** our **LORD**.* ***(No more tears, my baby and my beautiful sisters!)***

My daughter-in-law Lena White with my son, Vincent White.

ABOUT THE AUTHOR

Being an abused mentally, physically, and spiritually woman from a back wood plantation in Arkansas, life has been very, very, hard on every level. Experiencing any form of love was not a part of my childhood, teen years, neither doing my early adulthood. As a matter of fact, being "love" is still a fact about life I'm trying to comprehend and understand even as an adult woman with children, grandchildren, and great-grandchildren. (That I call my "heartstrings"). I can recall sitting on what was called "the morning bench," repeating something about loving Jesus, then being baptized in a lake there on the plantation where we lived at that time. To say I understood what it meant to be of the Baptist faith and to be a Christian at that time would be a lie.

Nevertheless, when I was re-baptized after joining the Church of God in Christ fellowship (my experience was just with this one church, it has no barren on the COGIC Ministry as a whole) and became what was referred to as "sanctify" in the fall of 1985; brought new hope for finally receiving some type of love. I thought that I had finally got this "GOD" relationship thing right as I watched and listened how the people in my new church acted doing our church services. Surely, I would now begin to be loved since these people were living what I felted, was more holiness than I had ever seen. But sadly, that wasn't what happened to me. During those days, I wasn't aware of the difference between men's ability to use GOD's word to accomplish their own desires and GOD's ability to lead and guide through the Holy Spirit. Coming from such a dysfunctional background helped to make me a "prime candidate" for a life of confusion and a great lack of understanding when it came to biblical knowledge. Even though all that was true, I still had questions about how GOD had anything to do with what I was experiencing from that congregation. What I was being told about marriage and what was happening in my marriage at that time; began a "spiral" that I'm still enduring and will have to live with the rest of my life. I hope these facts will give some understanding about the mindset I had when telling the story about my life as I wrote this book. Hopefully, they will bring a greater understanding of why the biggest struggle of my life was learning to love and care for myself.

My joy in life came from being successful in pouring out my love on those I loved and cared about, "not getting love back." Becoming a cancer patient was just the beginning of my learning in this world one must never forget that above all, "fight the hardest for oneself!" Just to begin to start learning, that lesson only happens for me because of my cancer journey.

My 1st Born Takelia Ingram

(January 13, 1975 – December 25, 2014).

I would like to honor my daughter at this time within this book by telling her story of why she lost her life. This is the last photo my daughter took on Dec 21, 2014, the day before her scheduled hysterectomy surgery on that Monday. When I saw her last at her daughter and oldest granddaughter that Sunday, I questioned her again about maybe having the surgery done somewhere else due to her medical condition. I was concerned because the hospital in Blytheville, Arkansas wasn't as advanced as those in Memphis or Jonesboro, Arkansas. Alright, Momma don't start, she said. She assured me she had total faith in the doctor doing her surgery because he had already performed her last surgery that saved her life and stopped her from losing so much blood a few months earlier. This hysterectomy was needed to permanently repair the problem of her losing so much blood during her monthly cycle. I back down with my concerns. Maybe I'm just being my overprotected self, I thought. I hugged her and assured her that I would see her at the hospital after getting her sister to her doctor's appointment the next day. When I received the call from the hospital on that 22nd date of December asking permission to take my daughter back into an emergency surgery, my concerns were brought to life. As I requested why they were calling me for emergency surgery, the nurse informed me that my daughter was already headed back to surgery as we spoke, only saying she had a "bleed!" As I rushed to Blytheville emergency room, I knew that things were not good for my child. It was at 3:36 am that Tuesday morning, Takelia would open her eyes for the last time in this world and see me for only about 3 seconds (I counted each second) before she would close them forever. My child had her main artery behind her uterus nicked during that hysterectomy surgery. Her bladder had been torn in two different places, according to the Little Rock surgery team that had tried desperately to repair the damage that the surgeon in Blytheville had caused after she had been airlifted there. I had lost my child once again, but this time for good. I tried to speak beyond the grave for my child and bring it to light that she was the victim of malpractice. This doctor, who had saved her life once from a malfunctioning birth control IUD being implanted in her upside down during a surgery at this same hospital in Little Rock, back in October had now taken her life there at the hospital in Blytheville, Arkansas. I tried to seek legal counsel and help from the biggest law firm in Memphis, TN, but couldn't do anything as her mother because she was still married, even though they had been separated for over at least five years. When the statute of limitation came around on Christmas morning of 2018, once again, my heart was plunged into an overwhelming grieving consumption that I relive every Christmas since that happened. I now thank God again for Cancer that led to this book being public because at the least, I get to tell someone the truth about when I lost my 1st born for the last time, MY child lost her life at the hands of that doctor who caused her to bleed out due to her injures during that hysterectomy surgery.

INTRODUCTION

During the years of 2009 -2015, I found myself facing a battle for my life due to being diagnosed with stage 3 c breast cancer. My whole life was shaken. I lost all I had when I suddenly couldn't work my two jobs that brought in the money for all I did to provide for my family and myself.

During that time, my daughter-in-law had been diagnosed two months earlier with what they thought might be lung cancer that turned out to be breast cancer also. What I discovered was despite all the things that were being done for cancer patients' young and old, helping to maintain "everyday" living stability was not one of them. (This is where the need for Partnership Transformation Housing was born from and why all the royalties from this book are going to that business).

Especially for those newly diagnosed patients of the ages 40 – 61. I had just turned 50 years old and didn't have dependents at that time. Reality was for me, there was no help available through any agents other than the once every six-month assistance with a shut-off notice from the light, gas, and water company or an evidence notice for rent from this one organization in the town I was living in at that time. You could only get one or the other, not help with them both.

I have been a caregiver for at least 57 of my now 63-year-old life. I started at an early age caring for my siblings within our home on the farm years ago. I have cared for patients within healthcare faculties like a nursing homes, hospitals, rehab centers, home health, and private duties. I have dealt with all types of sickness, injuries, and diseases, from infants to grown-ups. I've been blessed by God to see people's health turn around in some of the worth conditions and then be the last face some have seen when they exit this world.

That included my precious oldest daughter "Takelia Ingram" in Dec. of 2014.

I have had a lifetime career of caregiving to so many different people of all ages. I have witnessed far too often the loneness and emptiness that many faces during an illness or during the ladder days of their lives. I was painfully becoming aware of the "displacement" and "overwhelming emotions" that one experiences when being told that you have a death treating disease and can't work and may not even be able to care for yourself anymore. As a "senior and cancer victim," I was now experiencing some of those emotions that I had seen as I cared for others. Reality was now staring me in the face as

I began my cancer treatments, which were, out of all those that I lived all my life for and had made what was more important to me than myself, there wasn't going to be anyone there for me now that I needed assistance. You see, it wasn't like they asked or required me to live that way. As I look back now, I recall one of my cousins in that abusive home we grew up in, asking me not to leave her, like all the other oldest siblings had left us behind. I can see now that it was at that time, I began placing others' welfare over my own and just never stopped. And living that way became more of my mindset due to my vowing that I would never let what happened to me and my siblings when our mother gave us away to Ms. Lee happen to my children when I became a mother. So, I just always placed the people I love, even the men in my life, and everything concerning them before myself and my needs. Now sadly, I had no one to do the same for me. Especially the man that I loved at that time. Little did I know that being diagnosed with "breast Cancer" would be the start to self-transformation that would come between who I had always been for others and force me to have to place my own welfare first. Because there was just no one else who could or would be there to help me fight that battle. There are so many lessons to learn about GOD in our life within my story that you, as the reader, are about to learn hopefully. It's due to those lessons GOD kept on me for the last 13 years about getting this book, not just published but getting this book out to the world. I have been through so many struggles to get this book to this point of being released. The LORD love and care for you that's reading my story so much. HE wouldn't let me rest in peace until this book got to you. I pray that now it is in your present the Holy Spirit lead you and guide you to complete deliverance in every area of your life that GOD has ordained to be healed, in Jesus Name. Amen.

"With tearful eyes and a humble Spirit, I truly, thank God for the results that my self-transformation journey of Breast Cancer in my life will cause in your life, after reading my story. Thank you for purchasing my book.

Table of Contents

OUT OF ORDER 15

FALLING FURTHER AND FURTHER OUT OF THE WILL OF GOD 51

WALKING IN THE FLESH 82

FACING THE RIGHT – CHOOSING THE WRONG 108

FACTS ABOUT MY HUSBAND BECAME CLEARER AS MY SPIRITUAL SIGHT GREW DIMMER 134

BACK INTO THAT SMALL WORLD 168

I CAME TO MYSELF 199

OUT OF THE FRYING PAN AND INTO THE FIRE 239

GOING BEYOND MY ABILITY 259

OUT OF ORDER

"Out of order" is the phrase that described my life for a long time before breast cancer was discovered in me in **April of 2009**.

I was diagnosed with two different types of cancers in my right breast, which according to my doctors, placed me in the **stage 3c** category of cancer. These cancers were located at both the 10:0'clock and 6:0'clock positions of that right breast. The only hope for me, according to them, was to remove the breast in hopes of eliminating cancer from my body. My mental state was locked into a do whatever mode because there were so many other things in my life that were more important to me.

As always, my family and work--financially taking care of my family; were the main things that stabilized and grounded me throughout my life. Nothing up until this point had happened to me, mentally or physically, to interrupt my feeling about that pattern. My right breast had always physically bothered me, but I had always lived life with pain in some form or fashion. As I reminisced about those days, I didn't know how long the pain had been there. But I do recall pain increasing within my breast, but I was sure it couldn't be cancer, not me. I would check for lumps in my breasts often because they were so large. I was sure I was okay. So, I neglected it and didn't take time out to deal with it.

I had one priority, which ranked as high as my children and grandchildren, and that was; making sure I didn't fail Jesus in my spiritual walk by committing the sin I feared the most; fornication or adultery. Those sins were some of the church's major topics and ones that I feared. Therefore, I would push for marriage with whoever the man was that I slept with. The other concern I had for marriage was trying to finically secure a better life for my children than I had experienced. I just didn't want to live with the thought of failing Christ, as I would be the way I had been taught back in sanctified church years earlier. Sexual infidelity outside of marriage had been embedded into my spirit as the worst crime that could be committed against God. *It's not easy to admit this, but I can't lie about this, no matter how degrading this fact makes me feel.*

Seven times I repeated marital vows (twice with my first husband), but it appeared to me that not once did I receive a *"husband"*. To go through all the details of what happened in those marriages would probably be enough material for another book. I didn't realize that my breast cancer experience was about to take me on a journey that would consume and change my entire life.

Breast cancer was going to force me to take a position, which would change my priorities to my children, grandchildren, and marriage. To say I was not ready for the demands that it was about to exact and exert upon my life is putting it lightly.

As I look back at this *"out of order"* period of my life, I can see how the very things that I didn't want to happen to me were the exact things that did happen within my life. My mind now goes to **Romans 7:19,** where the scripture states, *"For the good that I would I do not; but the evil that I would not, that I do."* Somehow, everything I was trying to make better in my life, without knowing, allowed Satan, either working through others or working within me, hindering or making so much worse. I failed to receive the results that I was working so hard over the years to obtain. **Ephesians 6:12** states: *"For we wrestle not against flesh and blood, but principalities, against power, against the rulers of the darkness of this world, against spiritual wickedness in high places."*

Past experiences played a significant role in how hard and desperately I would work to make a difference in the lives of the people I loved. My mother gave me, my sisters, and my brothers away when we were children. Whether she just gave us away permanently or had a plan someday to come back and get us, I'll never know. From time to time, I have heard bits and pieces of the story from my older sisters. And due to her being an Alzheimer's patient when she came back into my life, she was never able to explain her choice of giving us away to Ms. Lee.

My childhood was filled with cruel and abusive events from Ms. Lee that produced the grassroots of an *out of order lifestyle that was beyond my control of preventing.* I strongly feel now as though I didn't have a childhood due to all my cousins and I endured from that woman. You see, as far back as I can remember, I was responsible for the well fare of the younger siblings within the home we were being raised in, as I talked about within my introduction of this book. How I personally felt or any thoughts I had about my life during those years didn't mean anything to Ms. Lee, who was raising us. (We were raised calling her grandma, but due to the way I really feel about her now, I prefer to address her by the title; Ms. Lee). Ms. Lee had no problem embedding within my spirit that no one loved me or ever would love me. It's crazy to me *that even up unto recently,* I could still hear her voice: "You will never amount to anything in life, just like your *no-good daddy.*" I'm not sure who she hated the most; me or my Daddy? Maybe us both! Anyway, those types of statements appeared to be among her favorites to say to me as I grew up within that dysfunctional home. She seems to enjoy reminding me that my mother didn't even love me, and that was how she got stuck with me. (There usually were a lot of curse words within and between her statements, which I'm not going to repeat.)

She would say to me; that no-good daddy of yours just drives that truck over roads getting babies wherever he stopped. **(My daddy was a rolling stone as the singer's Temptation would sing).** No man would ever love a fat face ugly little (the word sounds like a witch) like you.

Then usually, a few licks to my head and/or those downgrading looks came right after those statements. But as I grew, I would keep doing whatever task she had me doing while she talked and physically abused me. How long each event would go on often would depend on how much liquor she had drunk at the time.

Over the years, it's sad to say, but I got used to it. As I got into my teen years, I found myself making more and more responses back to her statements, which would make her angrier, and then she would hit me anywhere she could with anything she could pick up at that moment. How much I talked back usually depended on how much liquor I knew she had been drinking.

I wasn't the only one she was cruel to within our home during that time. There were two of my cousins that she would do the same way. They both are resting in the LORD's love now. She had the ability to be kind, but only to my older sister above me and my brother that was born right after me (he and I had the same father). Next was my baby brother (at that time), whose father was one of her two sons, I think. And there was the baby of one of the three cousins living there with us, who I think father was also supposed to be one of her sons'.

It seemed to me that Ms. Lee and all the adults around us during those times were drunks. Some of my older sisters and my oldest brother had either run away, got married, or just left to get away from this woman.

It finally got to the point where I was the oldest left with six other people under me that consisted of cousins, brothers, and nephews. (As I talked about in my introduction). Of course, after being asked not to leave her behind by my cousin who had the same first name as I couldn't leave her in that home. I wasn't about to go anywhere and leave my little nephew anyway. He had my heart wrapped in his little hands. I took total care of him as though he was my son. The only times I was away from him was during school days and the summer months when I worked in the fields. Ms. Lee and the mate she had drunk far too much for me to feel at ease with the way they handled my nephew. There's much more to my life with Ms. Lee, but that would be enough materials for another book if I told that story.

But what I will say is that due to my upbringing experiences with Ms. Lee and my own mother giving me up at the age of four, my mind was already made up about when I started having my own children. I vowed to myself that I wasn't ever going to let them come up without the love that children should have from a mother. I much sadly say that I couldn't keep my vow with my first child, who is now resting with the LORD, totally healed from all life dilemmas in Jesus' Name. Being a young 16-year-old still bound under the authority of Ms. Lee when I got pregnant with her, I was totally helpless when she was just lifted off the sofa and taken from our dysfunctional drunken home that March Day in 1975 while I was at school. I was lifted in total despair that day after getting off our school bus and finding my child was gone. Broken and confused as to why this woman would take a child that she had constantly confessed in no way could be her son's child because he would never have anything to do with a drunk granddaughter who was so beneath their standard of living. Now my firstborn was right across the street, and I would no longer have her as my own, and Ms. Lee could care less about her being taken because she cared nothing about me. Ms. Lee only cared about the alcohol she and her mate were being provided in return of these women and the man she met regularly with at our drunken, dysfunctional house; she didn't care about my child being taken. This is just too painful now to talk about; this act was so out of order, but what could nothing like me do about it? My child was stolen. I desired to keep close to her; in hopes that she would know that she was my child and not her grandmother's. I didn't give my child away like my mother did me, but nevertheless, she was gone. That took me to a whole new place of just loving the people in my life even though they don't love you back. I loved her so, but I wasn't allowed to have anything to do with her being raised. The real story about my life with my firstborn would also be enough material for another book.

I much go on, with the two children that I did raise, nothing would stop me from being there for them even though he was the father of all three; he never loved me or them enough to help me raise them in any way. But then again, here was another person who I loved even without getting loved back, a pattern that had become a way of life for me, no matter how out of order it was.

Since there was so little order in my life, I failed at applying some "right order' within some areas of my daughters' lives. I was doing everything I could for them. No one came before my children, no one. I feel that I failed in giving my daughters "order" in some areas of their lives. When my daughters grew up and started to have their children, I was also out of order with the way I took on my role as a grandmother sometimes instead of getting back and letting them take care of their own children.

And in every one of my marriage relationships, I failed to let the husband, at the time, take his proper position as headship over the new family which he had just taken on.

And here I was now, with husband number seven. Sadly, I still allow that *out-of-order spirit* to have control in my life. Don't get me wrong; it wasn't like I knew, back then, all this information that I'm now writing in this book. What you are reading now is from a woman who has matured and has been delivered from those deceitful and destructive spirits. But at that point, I still had a very long way to go on my journey to sanity and stability.

I may not have known how to let a man take his rightful place in my life, but this invader called "breast cancer" was lying within, waiting to take control. It still hadn't become clear that this breast cancer wasn't asking for permission to invade my life. Neither did it care about what I did or did not get in life, or what I had learned or not learned, as far as it was concerned. Breast cancer was going to become the center focus of my life, whether I liked it or not. But, as yet, I still was clueless and unaware of what was about to happen to my life, as this invader was gradually, quietly and silently, invading my body and my life.

Until this invader appeared, the next biggest concern was the man who I was now married too. I felt that I was at the end of my rope with this seventh husband, even months before this invader was found. The year before we were married, my life with my husband Jerry was a happy one. After still desiring to have a husband as the bible taught, I began praying about a specific type of man in my life. Even though I had tried being married so many times before. Jerry seemed to be an answer to my specific prayer. We spent a lot of time talking about some of the failures with my prior marriages and his relationships. It appeared that Jerry and I were at the same point in life. We both had just recently moved to this city. We both were starting over with not many possessions, but we were happy and filled with faith that better times were ahead.

Jerry wasn't saved as the holiness church calls it or a member of any church when I met him. This holiness life was new to him, so he said. As I think about it now, instead of my first husband coming and joining the COGIC church I had joined back in 1985, none of the other men I married were members of a church when I met them. But after such a difficult time with my last husband, I had got serious in my prayer life for the next one. The one thing I had always been sure of was God hadn't given me all this knowledge about love for me not to be sharing it with someone.

I know many of you regular churchgoers have heard as much as I had about a man *should find the woman*, and the woman should wait to be seen. Well, that hadn't been the way I had gotten most of my husbands. But at this point in my life, I felt that I had learned my lesson. I was no longer searching or reaching out for a man, for me. I would allow my next husband to find me was my mindset.

I still hadn't realized this, but now I see that more deliverance from that marriage messes up back when I first joined that church years ago still needed to take place within my life.

Deep within my subconscious, silently lying, there was some damage from my youth playing its role in how I saw and confronted things in life. I felt I had overcome those negative words spoken over my life by Ms. Lee, but it's clear I hadn't. They were still working deep within my subconscious, keeping me captive to the false belief that *no man couldn't truly love me.*

Yet in life, I had become a great fighter at holding on to the belief that one day, God was going to prove her wrong. Despite all the laughter from so-called friends and even some family about the many times I had been married, I still believed that **married life** was the only life for me.

For years, I had allowed other people's thinking to cause me to make a lot of foolish decisions in my life. I was embarrassed and ashamed in some ways; about how my love life had played out over the years, not realizing that knowing true love was something I had grown up without.

But nothing was going to take away my faith and hope about the type of love God had given me within my heart. As a very young woman, God had revealed a revelation to me about HIS Godly love between a man and woman. This legitimate type of love was displayed when he created Eve from Adam's rib.

God revealed that to me, no matter how I had come to believe, my life was *out of order. Praise God!* Many times in my life, I often wondered why God would choose a messed-up person like me, with so much lack of love in my life, to reveal what true love is? Almost every time I wondered about this, this scripture would come to my mind: **Isaiah 55:8**, "For my thoughts are not your thoughts, neither are your ways my ways, saith the Lord."

This *revealed truth* about real love, which God had given me, was the reason why I couldn't settle for anything less, no matter how many times I had failed to receive it before. And it was apparent that I had failed more than a few times.

Looking back over my life, it is now apparent that I didn't have the right kind of love in any of my relationships; whether it was with a man, a parent, family, most friends, and even in most of the church families I had been a part of during my spiritual walk. But the coming invader of cancer would be uncovering that those "coming short of love" relationships in my life had not taken my belief away about the revelation of the **true love of God**. Yet, most who knew me had formed the false belief that I did not know about **true love** because of how my marriages in my life had played out over the years.

During my early days of meeting Jerry, he made me feel like my prayers were finally answered. During those days, he displayed the type of actions that he couldn't stay away from me. We had become so close that lying on the floor beside the sofa where I would often sleep was better for him, he said, than trying to stay away from me. We could work well together on any task- during the night, whether it was working with household issues, cars, reading, or discussing the **Word of God**. Jerry and I were so good together. We had such a oneness that people often told us we favor each other. I was asked more times than I care to remember now if we were sister and brother?

There were so many beautiful things about us when we were on one accord. And that type of oneness I never had with a man before. I responded to this man, and it appeared that he was doing the same with me. All these facts place such an important role with why I just couldn't let my marriage with Jerry go when the trouble started. I knew that it was different with him. I had humbled myself with Jerry in many ways that I never had before with any other man. I loved this man, and unfortunately, Satan knew how much.

So, he started to launch an attack against us. I knew it would come soon on this love the two of us were developing. Because in my love life was the same place the enemy had attacked me repeatedly in life. Satan knew that I was too sold out to God to give up on my spiritual walk. But he also knew my desire for a mate was strong.

Since the devil knew he couldn't get me to give up on God, he used the next best thing. For most of my life, I would mentally allow myself to be **worn out** in fighting to have the right love relationship with those I cared for. Satan also knew how hard I worked with those I loved; to protect them from *his evil assignments*. Long before I gave my life to Christ in August of 1985, targeting those that I love was Satan's go-to strategy against me. He had been very successful in keeping me so busy with the loved ones that I had little time to reach out to others; nevertheless, I was always listening and helping those that GOD would send across my path. I knew that reaching out to people to help them see and understand God's love for them was just one of my spiritual gifts from God.

I was sharply aware of my spiritual anointing and ability to war in the spirit for others who mostly were unaware of the devil's devises. I understood I hadn't just been called by GOD but also chosen. Another of the spiritual gifts that I was anointed was the ability to bring **God's Word** to life. And I loved doing it. At least one or more things was going to happen whenever I got the occasion to teach, preach, or discuss the **Word of God** with just one or many, almost always, someone got a clearer view of our Savior Jesus Christ, God our Heavenly Father, or the Holy Spirit. It didn't matter from whatever biblical text I was speaking about. Whenever the Holy Spirit would speak through me, someone or *the people I would be speaking to would receive more understanding and often a better ability to apply that understanding from* **God's Word** *to their life.* Most people would often say, "I never saw or looked at it that way before." This was my most consistent and favorite response.

My goal was, if God could work through me to get just one person to take **HIM** out of a religion box and open themselves up to him in a different way, then my work had been successfully done. I always knew that God was pleased with me when this happened. Pleasing God was the thing that I truly loved doing.

But I had an enemy who does his job very well. Working through those I loved had become a sign that Satan was at work trying to keep my focus on the fight to receive love, more than focusing on spiritual growth and reaching my rightful place in God's kingdom. This was the one thing that kept happening within my love life over and over.

All my spiritual gifts were at work in Jerry's life that first year of our relationship. The results where I thought: a man who had begun to love reading and to study the word of God like I did. Within Sunday school and in our bible classes, he was growing fast in the knowledge of God's word. I was sharing revelations with him that it took me years to learn and understand.

It appeared that it wouldn't take as many years for Jerry to grow spiritually as it had taken me. He seemed to enjoy learning about God and the different ways God worked within people's lives. Following the light of Christ within me, according to him, he has no problem doing. As busy as his work kept him, we were always studying and discussing God's Word together. I felt that God was trying to get Jerry to an intimate place within Him in less time than it took others. Back during that dating year, he would often tell me how he appreciated me and my knowledge of God that I shared with him.

There had been times when Jerry would seem excited about the fact of growing faster than people who had been in the church for years. He would often quote the phrase, "Now that's what I'm talking about." It made me excited to see how well he comprehended topics about God's Word when we studied together. How much he worked didn't seem to interfere with him taking time out to learn about God or me.

I knew Satan was going to try something, eventually. I warned Jerry about some of Satan's tricks when it came to those I loved. Separating him from me was a great possibility since he was getting so much understanding of God's word through me. Satan was about to not only turn my husband from his Godly ways, but the devil would turn him away from God and me.

As soon as we married that Friday night at our church, the last night of our winter revival, the separation began. Within the same hour, that same night. Little that I know then that the Jerry that came to church with me that night and had been in my life for the past year, I would never see or exist again. It was so incredible how swiftly it happened that I just now realized I couldn't assist the change because of how swiftly it took place. We would never be the same. I often tried to bring back to Jerry's memory his confessions about Satan's tricks. He told me that I didn't have to worry about Satan's temptations with him. He would even confess to so many other people in my life that my marital problems before were because I didn't have the right man in my life. Now with him, I did.

"Besides," he added, "I asked God to let me be an enhancement in your life, not a hindrance."

For three and a half years after our marriage, I would be on an up and down roller coaster, trying to get Jerry to remember what we had discussed while dating and who he had been to me, without any success.

There were a few times were doing those years that Jerry acknowledged that he did remember those prior statements he made. But he would never remember to the degree to cause him not to go back to being *the neglector he had now started to be in my life.* I was aware of why Satan worked so hard on Jerry's pride. If he had kept growing the way he did before we married, only God knew what he might have become spiritual.

A prophecy was given to him twice during those years of the marital battles between us. Twice, two different people had called him out doing one of our services at the church we attained and spoken to him the same thing. Both saints tried to explain *his unwillingness* to humble himself before God, but he would never listen. And it angered him and pushed him further and further from me when I would discuss his inability to humble himself before God; or remind him of his unwillingness of working with his wife, the way he had done when I was dating him.

My inability to just let Satan have my husband was why I kept fighting all those years for my marriage. I often would quote to him the same thing I did to my children and grandchildren, and that was: *I just can't let Satan have you.*

He would always turn and thank me for thinking of him that way. Those types of statements over the years made me fight even more to keep my husband. Time after time, I would try reaching that spiritual man I could see so plainly within my husband.

If only he would just let down that brick wall around his heart. I would beg him: *Just trust God's ways for your life and humble yourself under the power of God.* It was clear that if we followed God, there was no height we couldn't reach in HIM as a couple. A few times, as I have stated, he would realize he was wrong in neglecting me and treating me the way he was. And a few times, he even admitted his problem with humbling himself to God.

The few times he confessed his faults, he would always make the statement: "I know I am my own worst enemy."

The devil wanted me to admit that getting the man back that Jerry was before we were married was impossible.

I just wasn't ready at that time to give up on him because of the love and passion Jerry had shown me in the past and my love for God and His word. I often referred to Jerry as a ***great man of valor.*** I wonder now sometimes if I did see a great man of valor. Or was it just what I wanted to see in my husband. Was he that anointed man of God I had seen or was it just my wish for him to be it? I can't answer those two questions even now.

I sincerely believed Jerry to be that spiritual man I had envisioned him to be when we were dating. So, I begin to do things I had heard over the years which others had testified about when they had problems in their marriage: such as speaking those things that are not as if they were; and anointing his things: such as the house, his car, the truck, his clothes, his place in the bed where he slept and so on. I also anointed the chair where he had started to sleep in more than in the bed with me.

I anointed the tools he worked with at home and on the job. Yes, even the many pairs of shoes I had bought him to match every outfit he wore; I anointed with oil that had been prayed over by our leaders.

I often talked with my Pastor and First Lady about my marriage, seeking any help I could get. Only God knew how hard I fought for my marriage during those three and a half years.

I even forgot my embarrassment humbled myself even further, and went to others in the church for help. I talked with other leaders as discreetly as possible about my marital woes seeking advice on what to do.

This was hard because I would have preferred to keep our problems to ourselves. I was concerned when I talked to these people in our church about our marriage because it wasn't my intent to make my husband look bad. I went to two of my husband's deacon brothers on the deacon board with him and solicited them for help and advice. It had been over two years now of me battling with Jerry before I went to these men for help.

Since these men had been married for years, I strongly felt they could help us. I was not sure what their response would be. I had tried to seek help from spiritual leaders in my last marriage, but with no success.

But I had to try harder this time and fight Satan in ways that I hadn't before. I hoped that they might help me see my marriage in a clearer view and that they would try talking with my husband in a brotherly way.

God instructs those who are strong in the faith to reach down and help those who are weak.

Romans 15: 1 suggests, *"We then that are strong ought to bear the infirmities of the weak, and not to please ourselves."* I was becoming weaker and weaker, fighting to get back the togetherness that Jerry and I had once in every area of my life in our relationship.

He had joined this ministry with me before we married. And the members of this ministry supported us both. God had led me to this church. The Lord had worked for me to do there.

Was *I supposed to do that work with a husband by my side?* I didn't ask God that. I had been praying to be married to a good man, and Jerry was a good man.

Since we both were just coming out of other relationships, did either of us take time to allow God to show us anything or anyone else? Should we have taken more time? I'm sure there are as many answers to those questions for me as it is, hopefully, for those who are reading this book.

We did pray about whether it was God's will for us to be together...but as for me, *to be honest,* I didn't ask God for anything but for Jerry to be my loving spouse for life. As we prayed together about each other during our dating time frame, Jerry shared with me a revelation he was sure God gave him about us being together. According to Jerry, God had told him that I was his wife. And God told him *to follow the light* that He had placed in his life. Jerry was sure he was hearing from God. After he shared with me what God had given him, God dealt with me about him.

God revealed to me what He meant *"about following the light."* I was the woman that God had given him to be his wife, and Jerry needed just to keep following my experiences and my knowledge of HIM. Through our marriage, God could lead Jerry to his relationship with HIM; our Heavenly Father and Savior, the Lord Jesus Christ—and to a submissive and humbling place where God could endow him the more with His

Spirit.

I Corinthians 7: 14 read, "For the unbelieving husband is sanctified by the wife and the unbelieving wife by the husband."

During those troubling years of the spiritual warfare for our marriage, Jerry would no longer talk about the instructions God had given to him concerning sustaining the marriage.

And as I look back, it would be years later before he would be willing to address it again. It took the first year and a half of our marriage to get him even to admit that how he was neglecting me and treating me.

Jerry was very headstrong. The only thing he hated more than me bringing any faults of his to the light was me being right about those faults. *(I believe it was about this time he began to hate me.)* It was a hard thing to get him to admit his cruelty and neglect of me.

Both my mental and physical well-being had taken a beating just to get Jerry to the point of him agreeing that he was neglecting me. I was praising God that Jerry was finally admitting that he was ignoring me. But my praise was cut short when I realized that his *acceptance* wasn't going to stop his neglect or solve our problems.

After he admitted his neglect of me, the battle changed to one of me having to bring his neglect to light over and over. It was confusing to me how swiftly and smoothly he could go back to his neglecting ways. I didn't remember how swiftly he changed the night after we repeated our wedding vows; it was as if he never noticed what he was doing. Every ten to fourteen days, like clockwork, the neglect and bad treatments would start again.

His solution to the problem was that I should not let him go back to the place of neglecting me. (As if it was my responsibility to control his actions). "Just bring it to my attention," he would say. "Help me," he asked. He also included, "Knock me on the head or something. "And you know, the fighter in me tried just that. This went on for about another two years.

There was just one problem with the suggestions he gave: I would always have to experience the irrational man's cruelty that wouldn't humble himself before the levelheaded man with the solution would appear.

All the fighting was beginning to really take a toll on me. It was not just with him but also with the efforts I was exerting to help my daughters with their lives. At this time, my breast started hurting worse than it ever had. But being me, of course, I had to deal with my marriage and family issues first.

After all, I was that **superwoman** to everyone but myself. Looking back, I can see that I wasn't mentally ready, at that time, to let Jerry exit my life.

"No dating couple stays the same after they are married, "Jerry would often shout at me and speak.

"That might be true," I would answer, "but you changed and just stop cold turkey the night after we married…not a few changes, a little at a time, year by year. All your gentleness, passion, sexual attention, and gentlemanly ways abruptly stopped. You only pay me attention now when you are in the mood." He would then get mad and make me wait even longer before he would meet my sexual needs.

I knew tests were going to come for us. I knew they would take place in our marriage. But because of the strong unity I thought we had built during that year of dating, I could never have imagined us being where we are now.

All couples have some **ups** and **downs** because when two different mindsets come together, there is a clash of wills, but this didn't happen for an entire year before we married.

This was the problem we were having and would have until we separated. *Where did this mindset Jerry has now come from?* After our wedding day, I wasn't familiar with the person that showed up, and I no longer knew this man.

The only way we could have drifted this far apart in our mindsets was only if one of us had pretended to be someone different during the courtship period. (It was now bad; I mean bad). One thing that I was sure of, on my part, was that I loved this man in a way I had never loved any man other than my children's father.

It had taken years for me to get over my separation from my first husband. Neither my children nor I was ever satisfied with the absence of him in our lives. Now I was faced with the possibility of going through a hurt even more significant than that, and my heart couldn't accept it. So, I was determined to do everything I could. I just couldn't let Jerry go. But his attitude and his coldness only got worse. The laughter and sweetness that used to be a part of our conversation, we now had lost. Jerry's *inability to stay away from my attitude* had now turned into one of him working later and later to avoid my presence.

It appeared that the devil was winning, and to tell the truth; I was tired of fighting alone. It was going to take us both fighting together against a familiar foe for us to save our marriage. The three-and-a-half-year effort to get back the man that used to work so well with me had become too much of a problem.

I had no idea that an invader **(breast cancer)** was, at the same time, also working on my weary and worn-out body.

Jerry and I were arguing about things that didn't make sense for two people who both were claiming Jesus as their Lord and Savior to be at odds over. I hated what the two of us had now become and how our marriage was failing.

I still loved my husband. ***The fact was:*** my heart and my body didn't change when Jerry changed in the way he treated me. I always warmly responded (when he would physically touch me) with anticipation and with love.

I will not lie and say that my failure with Jerry was only in one area of our married life. One of my most significant failures was seeing what Satan was doing to my husband's spiritual life. I was fasting and praying at that time, but my pain wouldn't allow me to hear any answers from God. I was so focused on not letting Satan have the man; I fought the battle in my strength and wisdom, allowing Satan to set a stronghold in my own life.

I was insistent on making Jerry see how he was being tested. So insistent that I couldn't see how far I was getting out of the will of God in my own life and how I was failing my spiritual tests.

I was hurting, and that hurt was making me so angry. My fight was with my husband's flesh and blood when it should have been with spiritual foes in high places. I knew that and GOD knows I tried, but I was becoming so weak from what was going on inside my body that I didn't know about.

As I look back over my life during that season, I remember how my breast would hurt. But since my heart was aching and hurting even worse, it was easier not to deal with the breast pain and ignore it.

Jerry wasn't the only one who was changing at this point in our marriage. I was now making more and more decisions from my flesh that was wearing out, ignoring my **born-again spirit man.**

Rom. 8:5 says, "For they that are after the flesh, do mind the things of the flesh; but they that are after the Spirit, the things of the Spirit."

Before I lost all hope for my marriage, I tried something that I hadn't tried in any other marriages before. I called several different places that did counseling with married couples. From the phone calls, I found one that I preferred, which was *spiritual* based.

I desperately needed someone to help us make sense out of where our marriage was going. We needed a wise counselor who could instruct us in the way of God and could help us get back into God's will for our marriage and lives.

I thought that I had found hope, so when he came in from work, I immediately spoke to Jerry about getting counseling for our marriage. He had his back to me and was taking off his work clothes.

Jerry very rudely responded, "We don't have the money for anything like that," without even turning to face me as he spoke. He kept doing what he was doing. Then he added, "there's not anything wrong with our marriage."

"The only problem we have is you just needed to face the fact that I am not going to do anything different from what I'm already doing" The kind of love he was giving me and the way he was treating me, he insisted, wasn't going to change, and he was sick of telling me the same thing, repeatedly.

"I love you," Jerry said. "It may not be the kind of love you want, but it is all you're going to get from me. How many people get the kind of love you're talking about anyway?" he asked.

One I knew of for sure, I thought. That was the love I received from you doing the year we dated before our marriage.

I drop my head and I subject that maybe we should do what we had come so very close to doing just a few months earlier.

Which was: going our separate ways. Jerry had finally got me to the point of believing he meant what he said. But what he failed to see was: *this time, I meant it too.*

If I didn't get the man I had before we married (one that would at least try to work with me), I determined I didn't want a thing at all from this one. Everything within me had just **given out.**

I had just visited my doctor, and she had warned me that my blood pressure was elevated, and I couldn't take much more in the way of stress.

She also informs me that she wasn't happy with how my right breast felt to her during my last visit in July of 2008.

I didn't discuss her diagnosis at that time with Jerry; I had let my day job go and was only working the night one.

I had left my day job to spend more time with my husband. My health benefits had been with my day job and not the night one. But I was on my husband's insurance, so I felt *that insurance wise,* I was just fine.

But sadly, that was not the case. Just like I didn't know about the cancer taking over my body, I also didn't know my current health insurance status. My doctor's office left a message on my voice mail. They tried to make an appointment to get my breast checked out and found out that I had no insurance. I called to inform them that I no longer had the insurance with the company I worked for doing the day, but I told them to run my second card with my husband's insurance and then make the appointment.

They informed me they had tried that more than once, and it didn't go through. We discovered that in my husband's patterns of being busy with anything but me, he forgot to redo his paperwork at the beginning of the year to retain health benefits on me.

He had unwisely assumed that everything with his insurance would stay the same if he had no new changes. That was over four months before. It was July now, and I would now have to wait until the next opening in January of the following year for health coverage on his job.

My husband's lack of concern for me was not just in the way he treated me at home; it was now spilling over into the business part of our lives.

To say that I was *off-the-chain* in anger is putting it lightly very, very, very lightly. That out of-order spirit was at full force inside of me. In my mind, this latest blunder just added to the fact of how badly his neglect for me had become.

Now sadly to say, our marriage didn't have a chance. Jerry had now become an enemy to my physical-well-being. After this incident, I stopped fighting for the marriage and starting to fight my husband. Without his insurance being active, I had to pay for all the medical expenses out of my pocket.

My blood pressure pills alone cost more than I was making in two days on my job. My breast was giving me more and more problems with pain. But just like that funky attitude of my husband's, I could do nothing about it. I stopped going to the doctor because I just couldn't afford it.

"Jerry, you have to go!" was all I wanted to talk about with him. Months earlier, before we moved into our current home, that statement was just a warning to get his attention. But now, I was more than ready and willing to give up on the marriage. (At least, I thought I was).

Back then, we both knew that he wouldn't have a problem finding a place because he worked in the maintenance department managing the apartment complex where he worked. Little did I know, and wouldn't find out until about a year later, that he did get an apartment with the people he worked for; He just had never told me.

(Did I mention that he didn't have any problem with lying to me either?) I would have to be the only one who had to search for a place to stay when we separated, and he was aware of that fact.

I had found this place we were currently living in due to our plain to separate for good. I was so excited about this new place. I purchased paint and bought new furniture. And eventually, the house looked just like I wanted it. But I must admit, as angry as I was with Jerry, something in me still couldn't completely let him go.

So, in spite us supposing to separate Jerry ended up working on the house with me to make it nicer before moving in with me. Four months later, here we were threatening each other with separation again, but by this time, he had brought a dog home to live with us.

We were at a heated point in our relationship that had now escalated. That house was mine!!! And now he had brought home a dog. I was no longer that woman fighting for her marriage. I was fighting Jerry. "Just get out!" was all I could say. The lease was in my name, and I wasn't going anywhere. He didn't want to move out now because he didn't want to give up that dog he had showed up at my house with; without telling me about it.

He refused to address the fact that I was the one who had found the house and had put so much work and money into it. He assumed that by myself, I wouldn't be able to pay the rent. I wasn't worried about paying the rent because I had a great relationship with my landlord.

I knew that my landlord would work with me about the rent because he was well-pleased with the work and enthusiasm I had put into his property.

I knew Jerry very well, and I knew that he knew I was right about the reason I was fighting him for my rental house. Jerry was more willing to give me up than that dog. The fact that the dog was too big for an apartment was the main reason he didn't want to get out of the house now.

And if you remember, I spoke earlier about how strong headed he would get when I was right about anything concerning him or his actions. He knew I was right about why I was fighting him over this place that I had gotten on my own.

Our warfare got heated. I couldn't believe that he would allow me to go through all the changes he knew I would have to face in getting another place. I still felt that all he had to do was just let his employers know his needs. They would have no problem helping him by giving him one of the apartments he where he worked.

The battle about the house and the dog just made our fighting worse. How we spoke to one another was an indicator that we were far from letting the Spirit of God do anything through either of us. We both were still attending church, but we were far from being true Christians at this point.

Jerry often would quote, "I thought you were of God," thinking that I was supposed just to take and deal with anything he dished out.

Please tell me how many times the hell raisers in your life always try to use the "I thought you were saved" argument on you. More times than often, that phrase is used when someone is trying to just run over you. Then there's the phrase, "But you've been saved longer." This is just another form of manipulation used only God knows how many times.

Then there is the famous argument of *using one's position* in God. This one (I believe) is the most used of them when criticizing and condemning those in leadership positions within the church. But never, never (when dealing with a devil) is your position in the church used to lift you or give you the respect you should have with that position. Instead, it is always used to bring you down somehow.

During that time, I walked in the role of an associate pastor at our church we were attaining. Having that title (in Jerry's mind) should have meant that I was strong enough to deal with his attitude; and that I was supposed to accept his acts of cruelty and neglect willingly. From the way he would yell those phrases at me, it was as if those facts were supposed to make a difference in how I allowed him to treat me.

My arguments for Jerry were these: Since you agree I have been saved longer, shouldn't this mean I should be the one more like God between the two of us, and that it would be wiser for you to be following me instead of fighting me? My second point was this: You also have a title in our church as a deacon…why aren't you carrying out your role, while you try to use minds against me?

As a deacon, his role in the church should be taking care of business matters and that my role, as one of his pastors (which I was at that time), was to continue in prayer and in ministering the Word of God. **Acts 6:3-4** states, *"Wherefore brethren, look ye out among you seven men of honest report, full of the Holy Ghost and wisdom, which we may appoint over this business. But we will give ourselves continually to prayer and to the ministry of the word."*

"Please, let us not talk about the kind of head you have been these past three and a half years of our marriage. The only covering I have been getting from you as a husband is an abuse by the Word and sexual neglect."

I Corinthians 7:3-5 states, "Let the husband render unto the wife due benevolence: and likewise, also the wife unto the husband. The wife hath not power of her own body but the husband: and likewise, also the husband hath not power of his own body, but the wife. Defraud ye not one the other, except it be with consent for a time that ye may give yourselves to fasting and prayer; and come together again, that Satan tempts you not for your incontinency."

I went on in my argument with my husband: "You have been negligent in every area those scriptures talk about. Do we really want to keep dwelling on this **title thing** in God? Since you want to use **my title**; what about a Deacon disrespecting and treating his wife in so many dishonorable ways and then blatantly confesses; that he's not going to change. Jerry, you're also dishonoring me in my role as one of your **associate pastors.**"

I Chronicles 16:21-22 admonishes, "He (God) suffered no man to do them wrong: yea, he reproved kings for their sake. Saying, Touch not mine anointed, and do my prophets no harm."

I disputed further, "While you want to use my title against me? Do you think God's rules are different for me as an associate pastor than they are for you as a deacon?" It was clear that my title in the church didn't mean anything to my husband unless he could use it against me. *As for his woman, his helpmate, his spiritual light, and the wife he was supposed to love until death do us part, what happened?* Concerning those issues, Jerry refused to open his mouth.

I protested further in my anger: Don't you remember: I am the woman that only issues in her prior marriages according to you, was she just hadn't married the right man which was you? And what happened to all that stuff about how you wanted to enhance me and not hinder me? And what about your powerful prayer to God: **'Lord, makes our marriage an example for other couples'?"**

"Don't you remember when one of the greatest women of God I have been blessed to know spoke a word from God to us? What about the **word** she gave you telling you about how God was still trying to heal that little girl trapped inside the woman he had now made you the head and covering over? And that you could be the one who could help Him in this healing process."

I argued, "You know, man, I am (the same women) who you confessed God told you was your wife. Then there's the letter that God wrote to you through the power of the Holy Ghost. Maybe, just maybe Jerry, if you hadn't showered me with all that love and affection before we were married, I wouldn't be looking for it now! Remember how you preached that *what it takes to get someone, it takes the same thing to keep them.*"

As I look back now reminiscing, I'm thinking to myself: no wonder he would use neglect on you; it wasn't anything else he could do with you, with your fly-month self.

Even though I was right about what I said, I sure wasn't in the right spirit when I said it. I just took things too far.

My past was always creeping up to remind me in the words of Ms. Lee, *'I told you, no one would ever love you!'* But she was wrong. Someone had loved me for a whole year of dating. And that someone lived somewhere inside of Jerry, and I wanted him back!

When I would become disappointed, angry, and would threaten to move out, the only thing Jerry had to do was at least try to calm me down or comfort me rather than always respond with those insensitive words: *"If you want to leave, leave. I will not force you to stay."* It would have also helped our marriage if my husband had not kept insisting that he wasn't going to change or give me anything more in the union.

"I may not love you as you claim I did before, but it's all I'm going to give." Then he would add, "Just deal with it."

But how could I? My love for this man gave him a place in my heart that neither my Heavenly Father nor my Lord Jesus had at the time. Even though I didn't realize it.

Yes, my life was still out of order, but an invader was about to take me on a cancerous journey that would break into little pieces; everything within my heart, mind, body, and soul.

Only my Heavenly Father, and my Lord Jesus Christ, through the Holy Ghost, could restore the **right order** to the disassembled and fractured portions of my shattered life.

FALLING FURTHER AND FURTHER OUT OF THE WILL OF GOD

Have you ever been in a church service where the speaker, usually the pastor, speaks about how a couple who had just got out of the car fighting composed themselves and walked into the service as if they were the happiest people in the world?

Usually, a statement like this brings an outburst of laughter from the whole congregation. Jerry and I were involved in one of these heated arguments on the way to a service at our Bishop's church one Sunday. Instead of it being funny, when it happened to us, it was excruciating.

Another week had passed, and Jerry was neglecting me again. Suggestively, I was still trying to *bring this to his attention.* We had discussed it during our last make-up session, and he had promised to try harder to be sensitive to my needs. Just as it was his custom, I was right back dealing with the same Jerry who had refused to hear anything negative about himself. In anger, Jerry hit the dashboard of the car and yelled at me bitterly. (I won't repeat the words he said). But what he said left my spirit crushed.

When we arrived at the Bishop's church, I was having a tough time faking being alright. As bad as I wanted to sustain my marriage, my body, mind, and spirit were just not able to go any further. It was clear that all Jerry wanted me to do was take whatever he dished out and accept his dirt like a floor mat.

God will not do the one thing to go against a person's will and push something upon a person that the person doesn't want. **Revelation 3: 20** states: "Behold, I stand at the door, and knock: if any man hears my voice, and opens the door, I will come into him and will sup with him, and he with me."

Jerry's *will* was fed-up, and so were mine. He yelled before we got out of the car, "I'm doing more for you than I've ever done for any other woman in my life."

I yelled back, "That's not true! The woman before we married got much more out of you!"

I was sick of arguing about his action and the house.

Over and over, he kept reinforcing his words that he *wasn't going to love me in any different way than the way he had been*. I knew it was now time to start deciding to move out. Instead of doing what most men would do to hold on to their wife, Jerry displayed his same cold attitude while mentally pushing me away.

I was angry that this man was driving me away from a house that I had invested so much money, time, and hard work.

The next day, I called my pastor and first lady. I wanted them to know what I was about to do. They had some business to take care of, but they invited me to ride along with them. As we rode around that day, I poured my heart out about how my marriage had gotten to be more than I could physically and mentally take.

From that day's conversation, my pastor reminded me that women in today's world and church don't wait until a man is divorced to come after him. In this statement, he warned me that women would go after my husband as soon as they knew we were no longer together. By now, I was well knowledgeable of this fact.

Jerry had refused to humble himself or work with me in any way, so I felt I had no other option. I could hear his harsh voice in my ear, resounding like the woman who had raised me: "Leave if you want to and watch and see if I try to stop you.

Go!!! It doesn't make me any difference."

The one thing I had going for me at this time was the *never-ending love* that my pastor and my first lady consistently showed me. (Finally, for the first time, I was receiving the right type of love from my spiritual leaders: the agape, unconditional love of Christ.)

All along, the pastor and his wife had been helping me as much as they could. But the devil just never stopped coming at me from every direction, and by now, even they had noticed my sad situation. My awful marriage situation had escalated, along with all my other problems.

Sadly, my pastor and his wife weren't seeing the right spiritual actions from either Jerry or me that would make a difference in saving the marriage. But they kept talking to me and praying for us both during those years. They both knew how hard I had worked, trying to hold on to my husband. Even now, they could discern that I still loved him despite what was coming out of my mouth.

When we pulled up in my driveway, my pastor turned, looked in the back of the car where I sat with my head down, and he began to speak, "I'm going to tell you the truth, pastor simply. First, I don't know how you're handling all the blows coming at you." Secondly, he said, "I have never experienced anyone, in all my years of ministry, with as many spiritual attacks as you have come at them at one time." Since the pastor didn't know how to help me any further, he suggested that I talk with our Bishop. But I was too worn out to fight for my marriage any longer.

Once before, I had faced almost this same situation in marriage. The pastor of our former church that my ex-husbands and I were members of; wouldn't even attempt to sit down and talk with us after informing him that our marriage was in trouble.

That pastor's response was this: "As a minister, you should know what to do."

Maybe, he felt, that as a minister, I should have known the answers, and perhaps he was right. Nevertheless, I was still a human, and the truth where it takes two people working together when it comes to keeping and maintaining a good marriage. It may have appeared to that pastor that I should have been able as one of the leaders in the church to handle this along, but to me, he wasn't concerned that the devil had come up again me in this area of my life more than once and I wasn't able to not end at the door of divorce, and he knew this.

Just as my pastor at that time had an opinion about me, I also had an opinion about him. I believed that a spiritual leader should be there for his members to guide them during battles, no matter what areas of their life those battles were in. (But once again, that would be enough material for another book.)

I became disillusioned and very disappointed with the unwillingness to give me any direction doing that with my marriage at that time from my leader. When the Holy Spirit led me to leave, I was sad to leave my son behind and my marriage at that time, but I wasn't that Ministry. I then relocated to the state I was currently residing in currently. After I moved, that pastor was among the first to speak doom over me for relocating. The intimidation and badgering got so cruel and intense from some of the Ministry's spiritual leaders of that church that God himself finally moved on my behalf and dialed with the direct source. He used that pastor's father, who was also our Bishop at that time, to help me.

I was really going through torment about should I have left. It was beginning to overcome me getting so much negative treatment from some of the leadership due to them siding with my husband since he was still attending their church. So, I was traveling back and forward from my new resident to where my husband and son were staying. During one of my visits there, that pastor and some members were working on the new church they had purchased. I was helping them while I was there and enduring what was being said to me about me being out of order for leaving my husband at that time. Even though my husband knew that the reason I had left was because of some serious issues about his supposed to be ex-wife and some things he wasn't about to change with their family. God had revealed that he was still married to her, and I could only be looked at as the second wife in the state of Illinois. She will receive all his assets if anything happens to him, not myself. He wasn't revealing any of this information to our leaders. Neither did I because I felted, he should be the man and step in and handle this situation. But he didn't, instead, he just set back and allowed me to be tormented by these people keeping himself looking like the good guy that he loved so much being in people's eyes. While this was going on, I just kept helping with the remodeling going on that night. Then that pastor had received a call from his father. Without knowing what God was doing, the pastor brought me the phone and instructed me that someone wanted to talk to me. Clueless and somewhat afraid, I took the phone. It was his father and our Bishop. "Girl," he asked, "what are you doing in that city?" I couldn't speak for being in shock. "Get on back home; I need you here," he said, and I replied, "Yes, sir."

As I gave the phone back to that pastor, he asked me, "Do they need you that bad down there?"

I answered, "I guess they do."

For months, after obeying my Bishop and returning down south, my then-husband and I kept in contact. As he and I would talk back and forth on the phone, he would tell me just what my former pastor said about me and how people in the church matched him up with other sisters in that Ministry. My estranged husband loved tormenting me about the church sisters not having a problem letting him know they were interested in him. Yet, he still was dedicated to his daughter's wishes and not going on to straighten out our marriage problems due to him still being married to her mother. Since he and I had gotten married in Tennessee, their law deems our marriage not legal. So, he just had to divorce me in Illinois so his 1st wife would be free to get his assets if anything happened to him. Since he had everything in his daughter's name, he took the sets to just devoice me in Illinois.

Having obtained prior experience and knowledge with how the sisters go after men in the church, I understood something similar would happen again to me with Jerry. But this time, I had someone in my corner. My pastor and first lady knew how hard I had tried to save my marriage with Jerry. Throughout my ordeal, they had given me their love and support, and they still believed that God had great plans for me and my life.

They both assured me that they would always love me and support me no matter where I went, and thus far, they have kept their promise.

When they told me this, it was as if they knew that I would face even more challenging times. But they were trying to relay that they would always be there for me. Of course, I didn't see all this then.

The **invader, breast cancer,** was silently taking a toll on me that I wasn't yet able to access. At that time, no physical pain was more significant than that at the door; I was about to enter once again, called; "another lost marriage."

In my conversation with my pastor, I told him and his lovely wife that I had to give up my associate pastor duties. They told me that the Holy Spirit had already informed them that I would do this. I concluded it was best so Jerry could wake up and try to become closer to God by walking in his position as a deacon.

My first lady looked at me and smiled. She had picked up on even what I couldn't see now: *Even now, I was more concerned for Jerry's spiritual outcome than my own.* "You're going to be all right, Pastor." She spoke to me, saying with confidence,

There was one thing my years of being saved had taught me, and that was this: *I could make it in any church that God would lead me to.* (What I didn't see was how far I had gotten from letting the Holy Spirit lead me.)

Even though it appeared that our marriage was over, I still had hoped for Jerry to become a great man of God.

My prayer was for Jerry to humble himself and confront the troubled areas of his life with tenacity and faith; instead of running or taking the easy way out.

John 16: 33 states, "In the world, ye shall have tribulation: but be of good cheer; I have overcome the world."

Rom. 5:3 says: *"But we glory in tribulation also: knowing tribulation worketh patience; patience experience and experience hope."* Life with Jerry had not only made me forget these beautiful words, but it had also taken me away from one of my greatest passions which were opening my bible and searching the word of God.

Rom. 12:12 encourages us with these words,

"Rejoicing in hope; patient in tribulation, continuing instant in prayer." I wasn't close enough now with God to partake of any rejoicings, and my prayer life had now faded to naught.

I had nothing left within me. I could no longer keep trying to get Jerry to remember the ensuing dangers that God had forewarned him of during our courtship period.

My poor husband had not remembered the warnings that came when he first got saved. The Lord gave the word about how He would eventually take the infant-stag hedge from around him so that he could spiritually grow up. God would remove the hedge from him, not because he didn't love Jerry, nor because HE didn't know what Jerry was going to do.

But as parents must sometimes let a child go on their own to give the child space to learn and grow; so does God with his children—just as HE did in **Luke chapter 15** with the prodigal son, whom HE so graciously and patiently allowed to go into a far country.

I couldn't see or realize this back then. I had not only lost faith in the marriage, but I had also lost faith in God, being able to humble a man who was unwilling to humble himself.

I tried my best to get Jerry to see that our marriage's problems were only God allowing the two of us to grow. If he would only arise to a level in faith to wholly follow God, the Spirit of God would lead him to that place within him where that great man of valor lived. My fights and augments with Jerry wouldn't allow me to go to the place that God had for me in the spirit realm either (that place of victory and peace).

My self-will and spiritual rebellion were only pushing me further and further from the will of God in my life. I felt that Satan working through Jerry brought everything I had worked so hard for, during those four years of my life, to an extreme and inevitable end.

God knows I had been much better to Jerry than I had been to any other man. I was so angry at the fact that I was giving up on my marriage.

To be real and honest, even at this point, I wanted my home, I wanted my church, I wanted my pastor, and I wanted my life as Jerry's wife. I wanted my man back. But now, I was symbolically standing there, watching everything that meant so much to me, dying slowly, feeling as if I could not do anything to stop it. I had been at this place before when my 1st child was just taken away from me. I still have the residue of that experience working against me with her now as she had grown up believing I gave her up when she had been taking from me, and I felt I could do nothing about it. I could do nothing about how out of control my relationship was when my mother gave me up to Ms. Lee. I could do nothing about how my relationship had placed out with her father, my 1st love. I could do nothing about my ex-husband still being married to his 1st wife. Here I stood again, losing someone I loved that I could do nothing about.

I stood there, hopelessly watching all of this unfold in my life, not knowing how to trust in God's word. **Psalm 46:10** wisely admonishes us with these words: *"Be still, and know that I am God."*

At the thought of losing all those things I treasured in life, I became angrier and angrier each day.

A verse in **Romans Chapter 7** reads: *"So with the mind, I serve the law of God; but with the flesh the law of sin."* I found myself in the flesh, fighting Jerry instead of the devil, and I could not see the evil I was allowing anger to cause me to do.

Anger was pushing me more and more from a godly mindset to a fleshly one. **Philippians 2: 5** commands us to: *"Let this mind be in you, which was also in Christ Jesus."*

I had often heard people ask others, "What happened to push you to the breaking point?"

For me, I think it was the day after my talk with our pastor and first lady, the day I resigned from all my duties at the church. But even after that day, I didn't give up. Even though my hefty work schedule was from seven p.m. until seven a.m., my problems remained on my mind.

My adversary, the strong man, had sapped all my power to fight, I thought. But I would later find out that I still had more fights than I knew.

Whether Jerry remembered or even cared, I still had that sexual thing within me that had controlled me for years.

Since he wasn't doing what I needed him to do as a husband, the old man inside me offered suggestions.

I found myself entertaining this thought: "Why keep fighting with Jerry so hard to get him to meet your sexual needs…why not just let some other men do what he won't do with you. After all, with as much time as you have alone, it wouldn't be hard to commit adultery and get away with it…." I had been fighting this ungodly thought for years.

For three and a half years, Jerry only would have sex with me when he felt like it. He probably will never admit this but neglecting me sexually was perhaps his way of showing me that he was in control.

I heard that voice inside saying, "Over three years is just too long to beg someone to love you or to make love to you, and they do it only when they want to." Then my mind proceeded with this thought, "And why should any woman have to remind her husband, he had duties to his wife?" Not only had I gone through the embarrassment of reminding Jerry that I had sexual needs, but I also had to argue with him when I reminded him. Frankly, I had changed somewhat. If I had been the lady I was in the past, I wouldn't have shown the patience to get someone to love me the way I was now doing with Jerry. That old out of order Joann started to rise in me.

That old Joann usually would try for a while to put up with a man's neglectful ways, but if a man continued to do his own thing as Jerry had done over and over, that old Joann would say, *"Bye!" Baby momma would just let you go!*

Finally, that little spiritual mind I had left tried to kick in: You have come a long way from being that woman you were years ago. What good has following the thoughts of that old Joann done for you in the past?

During our courtship period, Jerry and I had discussed how I wanted all my marriages to work. And more than often, I would ask him if he was sure marrying me was what he wanted to do.

Due to the many different failure unions I had already experienced, I felt prudent to be concerned. Over and over during the engagement, Jerry would assure me that God had told him that I was his wife and that he was sure marrying me was what he wanted to do.

He assured me that he didn't want to have to ever go through looking for another spouse. He then asked me: "Where is your faith, Joann?"

I wish now I would have sought my Savior God for answers and had been more interested in God's will for me rather than mines and Jerry's.

Since I trusted Jerry and his seemingly sincere promises, what was happening to do those years of fighting was confusing and didn't make any sense. It was crazy. Because with this man, I believed I had followed God's direction. This time I did not go out looking for a man; the man had found me (I thought).

When I left the church, my last husband and I were in, and I came back home to work with the bishop and was in the process of finding a place to live; I met Jerry. While I was rushing to work one day, Jerry called out to me. The courtship with him had begun.

For years, I heard the biblical verse that says: *a man who finds a wife finds a good thing.* I had read this verse and studied it in **Proverb 18:22.**

For the first time during my years of desiring a husband, I had let the man find me. I was sure that if I followed what the bible taught about allowing the man to see me, my marriage would finally be a successful and lasting one.

This time, it was Jerry who kept pursuing me and kept making himself noticeable to me. It was Jerry that made the first move. It was Jerry who made himself available for whatever kind of help I needed.

He had at least one other woman who I knew was interested in him in our apartment complex. And he was forever on his phone arguing and talking with the women he had left back in another city he lived in before he moved to this one.

It was evident to both Jerry and me that he had other choices when choosing a woman in his life.

And being a new man in town, he would eventually encounter many more women interested in him, for sure. Even when he joined my church, I explained that women's choices would be just as plentiful with the sisters in the church as it was with the women in the world.

I let him know that he didn't have to choose me or my way of life. But according to Jerry, I was the one he was sure he wanted.

Jerry had a saying that he would quote over and over: "The same thing it takes to get someone, it takes the same thing to keep them." According to Jerry, he would not be like my previous husbands. He would be one who would always cherish me and treat me right.

What convinced me that Jerry was for me, more than anything else, was his assurance that God had told him that I was his wife (He had found me).

Now Jerry was pushing his wife away. I still wasn't ready to give my husband up. I broke down and shared the troubling thoughts about getting another man to do what he did too little of with my husband. I needed his help, and I was honestly and boldly pleading for it.

I Corinthians 7: 5 read, "...and come together again, that Satan tempts you not for your incontinency."

Ephesians 5: 25 admonish, "Husbands, love your wives, even as Christ also loved the church and gave himself for it."

When I shared with Jerry my troubling thoughts, he looked at me and laughed, then turned and went back to watching CSI on the television.

That was it! Oh, the *humiliation!* I couldn't take it anymore. I didn't try again.

There was a "friend," as today's women call them, who I had run across earlier that spring. We had occasionally been talking since I was alone so much. I knew this man before I met Jerry. He had always been very open about how he felt about me. I never believed him and didn't know why. I didn't take him seriously.

But now, it was getting fascinating and exciting to talk with him on the phone. I made one of the biggest mistakes a married woman can make when she is having troubles in her marriage. In my overwhelming despair, I confided to this man what I was going through with Jerry, seeking answers and a solution.

These conversations with this man were only helping me to get even more fed up with Jerry, even faster. All those intimate feelings that Jerry had not stirred up in me in months, my friend was arousing in every conversation we had. That evening before I left for work, Jerry let me know that he would visit his family that weekend.

I had been of every weekend from work, but Jerry had never tried to take advantage of that fact and spend quality time with me. But this friend was more than willing to take every advantage he could, to arrange timeout, to be with me. I had been battling to build up the courage to possibly take him up on his offer to be intimate with me.

My conversation with this friend was taking me to a place of thinking more and more that: "Yes, you can do this."

My mind joined in with; Jerry is not making any attempts to save the relationship or showing you any attention. Why not get someone else who will.

At this point, my spirit wasn't dead, and I wept bitterly at the reality that I was thinking about doing this. I could bring another man into our home and use our bed with him for what my husband didn't use anymore.

I buried my head in my pillow and spent hours in tears. The messed-up part about shedding all of those tears was that I didn't know for sure why I was crying. Was I crying because Jerry had pushed me to the point that I might be able to allow another man in his bed? Or was I weeping because I had fallen so far from God and that I was lying there, thinking such unholy thoughts, about bringing another man into our home.

As I look back at that moment, the real shame was: Although I had cried, my tears and sorrow hadn't washed away the ungodly thoughts of bringing another man into our home, out of my spirit.

After weeping bitterly, I slept for a few hours. When I awakened, I noticed that Jerry's lunch break had started. He usually took about an hour for lunch, and he almost always came home.

I knew Jerry so well I could tell you what he would do before he did it. He never strayed away from his usual routine when it came to me.

I still had a small amount of faith, and I was trying to believe that God would save my marriage. Being a romantic at heart, I always tried to think that Jerry was thinking of me during his days at work, as I was praying for him to do.

With that small amount of hope, I was encouraged, and I prayed, "God please, please, by some miracle, let him do something different for lunch today. Please God, give me a miracle, and let this man save me from myself (I should have been asking God to save me from myself)." I continued, "Please, let him show some sign that he wants this marriage as much as I do. God, let him break his usual routine today and not come home." Jerry's routine was to come home, walk back to the bedroom and look in on me, and then go and turn on the television to watch CSI; warmed up what I had prepared for his lunch or whatever he had picked up on the way...and feed the dog.

But Jerry did come home. My heart was racing inside of me as I heard him drive up, get out of the truck, and go into the house. Just like clockwork, he walked to the bedroom, looked in on me, turned back, and headed to the kitchen; then, he turned on the television.

I had promised myself after Jerry laughed at me when I told him about my thoughts of having another man; that I was through with him. But now, I wanted desperately to call out to him as he started walking back down the hallway to the kitchen.

But once again, I lay there hurting so bad I couldn't say a word. For once in our marriage, I needed my husband to make some effort to show me he cared for me, but he didn't.

As I heard him feed the dog, close the door, lock it and get in his truck to go back to work, I cried as if someone I loved had just died. It was as if he put the fatal blow of that pocketknife he had used for years within my heart.

I cried so much that evening that it seemed as though something within my head burst.

I now felt numb, as if I had no control at all. Someone had died, and that was the woman who loved a man more than she loved herself.

I prayed for one thing but what I got was *a woman who no longer had any feelings or emotions to deal with Jerry.* It was time to take care of business. And today was as good as any day to get started.

I pulled myself together, got dressed, and went and paid my rent for storage; for the first of August.

From that point on, I had nothing to discuss with Jerry. When I finally talked to him, he asked him if he was willing to help me carry what I wanted out of the house to put into storage. He replied, "Yes." At the end of the week, Jerry went out of town just as he had planned.

That Saturday afternoon, I sat outside alone on the front porch watching the cars build up at the house next door. A few of the men outside talking were looking over at my home, and they noticed me sitting there. They spoke to me, and I spoke back. I could hear a few responses from the group of men standing out there about how nice I looked sitting there. The idea crossed my mind again about getting another man to do what I needed, but I talked to myself out loud and said, "Girl, you can't do that."

An hour later, a call came in from "my friend." He asked, "Did Jerry go out of town as he had planned." I answered, "Yes, he did."

My male friend informed me that he was already in town and wasn't too far from where I stayed. "Should I come over he asked?" My body got weak. I didn't know what to say.

To break my silence, he came back with a comment of how much he had been looking forward to the opportunity to be alone with me. Sanity cried out within me, "Girl, you can't do this."

I begin to apologize to him, saying, I don't think that would be a good thing to do. He then began to remind me of all the things Jerry had been taking me through for the last months. Then he suggested, "Why not just let me stop over, and we just see how things go."

I agreed he could come over. Then, I walked around in circles within the house, like a caged animal trying to figure out where to go and what to do. In just a few minutes, as he said, he was pulling up outside. I was excited and disappointed at the same time. I invited him in, and as usual, we played cat and mice with each other.

He could see that I was nervous and confused. He turned to me and tried to make me feel more at ease. He began to talk to me. "Joann, you have a right to take care of yourself when he is refusing to do it for you. It's not like you haven't tried again and again to please him." He then took my hand, pulled me closer, and put his arms around me.

It felt good to be in his arms. He smelled wonderful, he looked wonderful, and he was just wonderful all the way around. Even though Jerry had neglected me, I still knew this was wrong. It was hard to allow myself to accept the passionate kiss from my friend. For a moment, my body started to agree with the pleasure and excitement it was receiving.

It wasn't hard for me to lose myself in his warm, strong arms. After the first few minutes of me just getting lost in the moment, something inside of me screamed and yelled: "What are you doing, Mrs.

Swims?" Ever since we were married, my husband and I would address each other as <u>Mrs.</u> and <u>Mister.</u>

When Jerry talked to me, he would say, "Mrs. Swims," and he would continue with what he wanted to say. When

I spoke to him about many things, I would begin, "Mr. Swims," and then I would go on with whatever I had to say.

Hearing this admonishing voice within, I stopped instantly and began to push my friend away. "I just can't." Tears start to roll down my face. "I can't do this. I know he's been a dog, but I can't. I just can't." My friend tried to get me to relax again, but it didn't work. He agreed to let me alone and pulled back. I was now ashamed and embarrassed.

I had tried, but I just couldn't do it. My friend, understanding this, just held me in his arms until I was able to calm down and stop crying. I thanked God that my friend wasn't angry with me. He knew that I just wasn't ready to move forward at that time. My mouth was talking, and my body was speaking to him loud and clear, but my heart wasn't agreeing with either of them.

He was so gentle with me. He stayed with me, asking me, again and again, was o.k. He pulled me back close to him after a while and said, walk me to my car. I did. He called me later that night and played with me in his humorous way, just as he always had done. He assured me that just because I backed out this time, it didn't mean that it wouldn't be another time and another chance. He reminded me that Jerry wasn't going to do any better and that Jerry wasn't going to change.

"That crazy husband of yours has lost his mind to allow so much woman to go to waste," he said.

I just listened as he talked, hoping even then that he was wrong.

Before I fell asleep that night, I lay in bed wondering about myself. *Who had I become? Or more like, what had this man awakened in me?*

Once again, I cried myself to sleep. Just as always, Jerry returned late that Sunday night. He prepared his clothes for work the next morning, got into the bed, turned his back to me, and fell fast asleep.

The next morning, as usual, he got up, casually spoke to me as he dressed, finished his morning tasks, and left for work.

Another week had passed with not one affectionate touch from my husband.

I spent that Monday morning packing up some of my things before I went to work that night. We both continued with our jobs and lives for another week, without discussing anything except: *Was he still going to help me move my things from the house.* He said, "Yes."

Throughout the rest of the week, I continued packing. Sometimes Jerry would get home before I left for work, but sometimes he would not make it home before working.

My plan was to be moved out of the house completely within a few more days. I had only told a few friends about my plan.

One of my best friends from my teen years was very concerned about me. She and some other ladies were going out to eat that Friday night, and she asked if I wanted to go.

It seemed like the best offer I had heard in a while. I agreed to meet them, and we were off. I didn't know whether to tell Jerry or not. He usually didn't come home until late, even when he knew I was at home. I waited a while for him, but eventually, I left, knowing that he probably didn't care where I went anyway.

That night, the ladies and I went to an **all-you-can-eat seafood special buffet** at one casino. The ladies I was with decided to look around before we ate.

Since I hadn't worn the best shoes for walking, I decided to just sit at the bar. It was my first trip to a casino. It turned out to be a very interesting night.

The music was live. It was a band. *I haven't heard a live band in years,* I thought to myself.

Who the band was, didn't matter. I loved to watch musicians play.

You can always tell outstanding musicians because they are one with their instruments. The magic between the musician and the instrument he plays is undoubtedly a talent given by God, no matter if the musician uses it to give Jesus the glory or not. I didn't know any of the songs those guys were singing, but the beauty of their talent and the way they played their instrument was great. I found myself having an unexpectedly good time.

A couple came and sat to my left at the bar. The lady started to ask me questions about the band. I told her that I had no idea who they were, but I was enjoying the sound.

The two of them were talking with me as if we all were buddies or something. I was glad to have the company, so I wouldn't stand out so much sitting there alone. It took me a minute to realize that something else was going on inside that bar.

I had been more focused on the band than my surroundings.

I heard the quote from a gospel song, "the devil knows how to do it!" **This wasn't a lie.**

You're talking about a fish out of water. (I was, in no kind of way, as they use to say: *back in the day*.) I was unprepared for the plan the enemy had for that ungodly thought he was subtly maturing in my mind: "What Jerry won't do, another man will."

Satan planned *to take control of my soul* (mind, will, and emotions). After I entered into his trap, it would take months before I returned to my senses, and his scheme was escalating with the events of this night.

Before I was saved, I would have worked the room by flirting and engaging with every eye upon me that night, but sister *girl* had been saved since August of 1985.

I've heard most people say in the church that it's not that you forget those things you did before you got saved; it's just that you don't desire to do them anymore. Those kinds of desires to "work the room" had died in me a long time ago.

I didn't have enough strength or willpower now to mentally pray for a way of escape.

My prayer life wasn't what it needed to be because I had neglected it. Honestly, my prayer life had faded as my marriage had.

I wasn't all that satisfied with God right about now. He had once again allowed me to lose so much by dealing with yet another insensitive man (Jerry). (Looking back now, I had no right to blame God).

I had strayed so far from God. And I'm realizing this even more as I am writing this book. Now that I think about it, for me to even notice what was happening at the bar. It was the move that one of the men around the bar made that woke me up to what was going on that night.

I enjoyed the musicians. My mind was clearly on the talent of the sweetness of the musicians' gifts and their instruments. All around the bar, different guys were checking me out. One of them finally turned around in his seat and just looked right at me. I looked, startled, trying to see what exactly had his focus.

I turned to my new friends and asked, "What is he looking at?" Her husband laughed and said, "You." His wife took a drink from her glass and turned to me and said, "Matter of fact, they all are looking at you."

I turned back to see just who *they all* were. One guy cleared his throat and replied, "Yes, I'm looking at you." I couldn't talk. "What are you drinking," he asked? "Coke," I answered. Then he asked, "Do you know that you are the most beautiful woman I've seen tonight?"

In my mind, I was like, hey, *I remember that line.* Then he said, "...with those bedroom eyes."

That made me pay a little more attention. I was thinking, "Now, how can you see my eyes in this light?" Back in my getting high and partying days, my eyes were one of the signature qualities I was known for.

Within my head, I was thinking, "Where are those girls who came with me?" We needed to be leaving to eat, right about now."

Little did he know, he had just messed up my appreciation and enjoyment for the music. I just smiled, not opening my mouth.

"Are you from here" was his next question. I just shook my head and silently said, "No." Then very slowly, I told him where I was from. He informed me that he worked there and asked would I take one of his cards. "Somebody comes and helps," I silently pleaded...Now, *what was I supposed to do?*

I took the card out of this strange hand that was in front of me. "Don't take the car if you're not going to call," he said. I gave him another smile.

Before I could figure out what to do next, another man was saving me from the aggressive one who had just given me the card. I had noticed this new gentleman when I looked to see whom my new lady friend was referring to when she made the statement, "They all are looking at you." I also noticed the guy with him who was a small man, firm in body structure. He reminded me of my first husband. The other reason I couldn't help but notice these two men were because the small guy next to the one that was saving me had been shouting out different aphorisms. The saying I recognized he repeated the most was, "Scooby Do!"

They both were light-skinned men. The one with the cap came closer to me as he talked. He began to speak to me about his business: He booked cruises for people.

He asked, *was I hanging out or what*? "Yes," I said. "But only until my friends meet me here at the bar. We're eating at the buffet tonight." Slowly his friend, who was firm and smaller in stature, came over.

The guy speaking to me introduced his friend.

I didn't focus on any names, but I noticed the boldness of his friend. We talked about the band. He asked was having a good time. "Yes," I answered. I think I spoke a little about how long it had been since I've seen a live band. I had no idea that these guys were regulars at this bar.

They knew I was not one of the regulars because they hadn't seen me around.

The devil was testing the water with me. He knew that at this point, he had to give me a reason to come out of that small world of mines before he could work on a possible trap for me. Satan had only one plan that night. He was causing these men to give me the type of attention I didn't receive at home, only to entrap me. I felt desirable again.

My friends found me at the bar where they had left me. But it appeared now that I had gained new friends. The couple at the bar was still talking to me now and then. The two guys who had come over to talk to me were still there too.

I mostly talked with the guy who booked cruises, but his friend stayed close by, chatting with what seen like everybody around him.

When my girlfriends re-entered the bar, I inquired they *were ready to eat?* "Aren't you?" they asked? "Sure, let's go," I replied.

Before we left, I introduced the guy who booked cruises to my girlfriends. I remembered the cruise guy's name because his card was still face-up in my hand.

The cruise guy was named John, and his friend was called R.B., whom we will refer to later on in the story as Mr. Intelligence. I introduced these two men to my girlfriends, and they all responded with "Hello." As we started leaving, R.B took my hand, kissed it, and said, "Enjoy your meals."

As we walked away, I remember thinking: He probably does this to all the women.

We did enjoy our meals from all the different buffet tables that night. I saw so many church people I knew there eating, and I observed that the *spirit of gluttony* was in full force.

It had been a while since I had been out with a group of ladies. I enjoyed myself, and it was an excellent chance to find an escape from all the battling I had been doing for the last few years with Jerry.

As I rode in the back seat of the car on the way home, I was thinking about Jerry, and the past four years I had spent with him. One reality went home with me after having received all that attention from those men. It was this: *My husband had been doing more than just neglecting my needs as his wife; he had allowed his selfishness and pride to neglect my womanhood.*

I began to now see how Jerry, through his actions, had been mentally abusing me.

In my youth and my earlier relationship with my children's father, I knew both physical and mental abuse very well.

It seems crazy now, but my thoughts were on which type of abuse was worst. From past experiences, mental abuse was always the worse for me. The abuser can't see the damage he or she does to the person they are abusing psychologically or mentally.

My relationship with Jerry had only added to the years of mental affliction in my life.

It was mental abuse when I had to fight Jerry to receive his attention and affection. And his derogatory words that often came along with those fights were also a form of mental abuse.

Somehow, I had been able to retain my passion-filled womanly qualities when my other marriages had ended.

But Jerry had managed to take it away over the year; he had mentally drained me.

As I now look back, I can see how I had let him take away my ability to enjoy even being a woman. But that was nothing compared to what I was about to go through.

The next day, I shared with Jerry about my evening out with the girls. The attention those men around the bar gave me was the part that I wanted him to hear. He displayed his usually disinterested and cold-hearted attitude.

"Well, it seemed as though you had a good time," he responded after at least five minutes of silence.

He had gotten good at demonstrating to me his "I don't care about your attitude" without even opening his mouth to say the words.

I could tell Jerry had work to do that day because he was loading his truck. After he finished putting the stuff in his vehicle, he said, "I'm leaving now. I'm headed to take care of business." Jerry then got into his truck and drove away without even touching or coming close to me. I took in a deep breath, went to bed, and I slept the rest of the day soundly.

WALKING IN THE FLESH

The week I was to move out and separate from Jerry finally came. When that dreadful Saturday came, both Jerry and I went about the day doing what was needed. I was cleaning, leaving a lot of my stuff behind so that Jerry could live comfortably in the house. Jerry had solicited a coworker to help him move the things I wanted to take from the home, and they went speedily about their business.

As the two of them worked, moving my things into storage, I went about redecorating the house so Jerry could still live comfortably. I cleaned the kitchen, living room, and that one-bedroom that he would be sleeping. Jerry didn't need it, so I left unhampered. He could only use it for storage space.

After I finished putting the house in good order for him to live comfortably, we talked about how he would help pay for the furniture I left him because I still owed payments on it.

I didn't put all my new furniture into storage for this reason: I wanted Jerry to have some nice furniture and a nice place to live.

That day was hard. I didn't want to go. But I was committed and had gone too far to turn around. I did a lot of crying for a long time after I moved out.

I didn't give up my keys to the house immediately because Jerry had allowed me the freedom to enter it whenever I needed to. I still came in occasionally to take care of his cleaning, and I even cooked meals for him.

Living without him didn't take its full effect on my mind, body, and soul immediately. Since I worked nights, it was really easy for me not to be at the house during the day. He wouldn't be there, and I wouldn't be able to see him anyway. For many months, Jerry, and I, unfortunately, had made this a routine, and it was our custom to be in that big house alone.

A few people asked me why I hadn't taken everything out of the house. It has always been hard for me to treat people how they mistreated me.

Even though I wanted to hurt Jerry, there were some things I still couldn't do. I have never been the type who could be low-down and dirty to others.

I had allowed the spirit of unbelief in my husband to take control of me. I could no longer trust him, and I no longer believed that he could treat me correctly. Only God knows how bad I wanted to believe in Jerry. But I couldn't trust him anymore; I just couldn't.

The thoughts of another man doing what Jerry hadn't done for me these many months seemed not to want to die. They kept bombarding my mind.

Other things were also occurring within me. Along with the *spirit* of fear that had entered my life came other spirits, like pride; vengeance; hurt; self-righteousness; hopelessness, and apathy. These spirits worked diligently together within me, causing Jerry and me not to join forces to fight for our marriage.

Matthew 12: 45 states, "Then goth he, and takes with himself seven other spirits more wicked than himself, and they enter in and dwell there; and the last state of that man is worse than the first."

These invading spirits hadn't just appeared with my moving out; they had been building up and trying to enter with every *cold-shoulder* Jerry had given me over the years.

I found myself now, as full of hell as Jerry was, or maybe I was even more entangled.

The reason I was so mad with Jerry was that I had given this man everything I had. And I had been a faithful and good wife to him, even better than I had been to my previous husbands.

I loved shopping for my husband. I would buy nice colognes and suitable clothing and shoes for all of my men. I took an interest in each of them, no matter their job or pleasure. I would always put their welfare before my own.

I took excellent care of them; spent endless time sharing the word of God with them. I kept their homes comfortable, clean and relaxing. God had given me the talent to be able to take a little of nothing, even things others had thrown away, and make myself, my home, and my family look like we were worth millions. My children's friends would often ask them if we were rich.

I believed that a man's home should be his castle. And in that castle, a king should be able to come home to a nice meal, a warm shower or bath, and the type of woman that could put back into him all that a stressful job and the outside world had taken away that day. I took this position with each of the men that I married.

But one problem always showed its ugly head. As I said earlier, not one of the men I married was saved. At some point in each marriage, my love for God would cause some problems with these men. According to them, the question arose either because I thought I knew too much about the word of God or because I loved God too much and would not take a back seat to their mess and would not tolerate the cruel way they treated me.

As I stated earlier, I got saved back in 1985. Each of the men I married would eventually come into the church through me. It was through my relationship with God that caused them to want to know HIM.

I loved living for God. I loved searching the deep things of the word of God. I always would get excited about any new fact that I learned about God. The many ways He would reveal Himself blew my mind.

All I wanted, when it came to a man, was someone that would share all those wonderful things I loved about God and would grow with me in God as we walked through life, side by side, worshipping him together. I needed a man for more than just to keep that sexual thing I had under control.

One of the greatest gifts in the world for me was to see all the beautiful works of God and the glory of Jesus and the Holy Ghost. O! Just to be given the gift through our Savior Jesus to love our heavenly father was a miracle. There was so much to share with others about this life with God. I felt that all I needed was the right man by my side to help me share it.

I knew *back then* that that uncontrollable sexual thing inside of me was stronger than I was. Instead of letting the God I loved and enjoyed sharing with others deliver me, I always looked for a man to marry me to fulfill my sexual craving, not realizing that I was trying to deliver myself-- when only God can *truly* deliver.

I believed that if I could just submit <u>all</u> to God and daily keep seeking his will for my life that even the sky wasn't the limit in where I could go in HIM.

Having a man beside me was sadly not only what I wanted but also what I believed I needed to get where God wanted me to go in life. I had this irrational and false belief that the man in my life didn't need to be saved when we married, but in due time, I thought my husband would be saved by being a witness to my faith and love for God.

I have seen a lot of hypocrisy in my life, both in the world and in the church. I have seen a few single brothers in the church who were church playboys. They knew that it wasn't hard to get women in the church, and it appeared that they would have their share of women in the world also.

Since these men knew that most of the single sisters in the church were probably looking for husbands, they eagerly took advantage of it *as a rooster in the hen house.*

I'm not concerned about how my readers may feel about my next statement because God in heaven knows I'm truthful. My opinion is: **There are just as many whores in some churches as there are in the world, both males and females.**

No matter what their race may be, women today may have set their standards for a man so low that the man does not have to bring anything to the table. No longer do men or women make a conscious effort to work together to produce and sustain a good relationship. The moment the first problem arises, both the man and woman are ready to give up on the relationship. Men and women are unwilling to work through their issues anymore, even when they believe they're with the spouse God has chosen for them.

I have seen selfish men in the church and the world, who appear to ask themselves this question: Why wait or work hard to obtain material things, which some women already have, and they are eager and willing to give it to us now.

Jerry became one of these men.

After our separation, both his walk with God and mines would drastically deteriorate.

Jerry moved in and was living with another woman and her kids. I confronted him about this, to which he replied, "How do you know that it can't be God blessing me to live in this woman's house to be a father and a male role model to her children." He continued, "And God could be blessing me through her." Then he added, "You told me that God wanted to use me as a leader!" He continued, "Those foster boys in her home love me, and they are excited to have me in their life. Why can't it be that God wants me to lead them?"

I wanted to hit him over the head when he made those statements. I wanted to hit him so badly; my head was about to burst.

Did I forget to tell you, when I heard those statements coming out of his mouth, I wanted to hit him. My thoughts were, "If I could just hit him and make sure the force from me hitting him was right in the top of his head, maybe, just maybe, he would realize how ridiculous those foolish words he had just spoken sound.

Since I couldn't talk any sense into him, maybe, I thought, the power from a lick in the top of his head would make something in his brain click.

Before I could hold myself back any longer, I angrily said, "Fool, how can it be God who is blessing you? How? How could it be God when you both are openly committing adultery in the eyes of God and before everyone around you? And what kind of leader do you think you are to those boys? Mentoring the children is one thing, but to move in with a woman and have sex before marriage was a sin. Don't you know those kids are not crazy? They know what the two of you are doing in that bed."

I went on, "Her young daughter already has a baby. What are the two of you reinforcing in her mind? Did either of you stop or think about how you are teaching this young lady that getting a baby out of wedlock isn't wrong how could it be; since her foster mother has another woman's husband in her bed every night?"

He then asked, "Do you think we were crazy enough to tell anyone in her life that I'm a married man?"

I couldn't help but to respond, "Do you hear what you are saying?" (I wanted to call him a "damn fool"), but I didn't.

But that did it for me. I thought to myself: Just let me shoot this crazy nut and bury him with the rest of the dead.

Many living-dead men and women are walking around on the earth. These men and women don't know God and don't want to know him. They think that they're free to do whatsoever they want to do and that it's alright.

I Chronicles 16: 9 informs us with these words: "For the eyes of the Lord run to and fro throughout the whole earth." **I Peter 3: 12** states: "For the eyes of the Lord are over the righteous, and His ears are open unto their prayer: But the face of the Lord is against them that do evil."

"God sees the two of you. It doesn't matter what anyone else knows or thinks", I yelled at him with all my might.

"You foolish dude," I then thought before I got a hold of myself.

After calming down my emotions, I begin to speak to him without the anger. "Jerry, God knows what the two of you are doing, and many of my relatives and friends know also. Also, your family and others in your life know that you're living with this woman. Don't forget, Jerry, that you are still a deacon. Some of the folks in the church where you attend probably know what you're doing too.

"No one may be bold enough in your life besides me to tell you," I continued, "but the truth is; since God sees the two of you, no one else matters. Has the devil taken total control of your mind, man? Don't you realize some people know what you are doing?"

When will people learn, even people in the church, that God cannot bless a person when they live a sinful lifestyle.

In Jerry's or my life, it wasn't God that had us doing what we were doing. It was our flesh at work, and we were doing what we wanted to do, even though we were misleading and hurting the innocent people who were on the sideline, observing the ungodliness in our lives.

When we had that conversation, I had just to calm down and back up off of Jerry. I wanted to hit him so severely.

The only difference between the two of us was I hadn't been foolish enough to think that God approved of and was satisfied with my backsliding ways. Yes, I also was guilty of committing adultery. But I wasn't crazy enough to think I could hide from God.

When I committed adultery, it was known to many around me at that time. I'm confessing this to my readers because it will not profit me to lie about this now.

I was an adulteress and a backslider, but I was still faithfully attending church because there was **something** on the inside of me that was stronger than I was at the time.

This **something** wouldn't let me enjoy what I was doing. Nor would it keep me from going to the house of God to plead for mercy.

I allowed myself to be overcome by sin and fall into adultery. I partly attribute to this: I had just had it with being faithful to disloyal husbands who would only abuse me and take advantage of my loyalty, love, and generosity. As I would give my all, they would capitulate nothing to the relationship.

No longer would I mentally and physically work myself to death to sustain a relationship with a man who, when discontented, could so quickly move on to another relationship.

A pattern had been established with the men that I had married. When a woman would show up with more wealth and more material things than I had, they were gone.

Suddenly, when that husband who claimed he loved me had a choice between a woman who loved God or a woman who had things, he would always choose the woman with everything every time.

Now Jerry, my latest husband and the one who had vowed that God had sent him to me, had done the very same thing.

I was finally tired of pouring out myself to those types of men. I had had enough of giving everything and receiving nothing.

I wasn't going to share the beauty of my God with any other man in the way I had previously done.

Once again, the devil had strategically sent men (wolves in sheep clothing) unto me; in hopes to drain me of my love and bereft me of my destiny and my faith in God.

The devil's intention for me was the same as it was for the job.

In **Job 1:11**, the devil told God: "But put forth thine hand now, and touch all that he hath, and he will curse thee to thy face."

I may not have been crazy or bold enough to curse God to his face, but indeed I had allowed those relationships with the men in my life to condemn Him. I had cursed God by being more concerned about having a man in my life than of doing His will.

My focus should have been on loving God and giving Him my all. I had cursed God for my lack of trust in Him and for not patiently waiting for Him to send the right man to me.

I had genuinely believed that with Jerry, my last husband, I had allowed God's will in my life. *Finally, the man had found me*, I thought.

Why had I now ended up in the same place with the man who had convinced me that God had told him I was his wife?

I know the answer now: I had prayed and sought God concerning HIS's will for my life. But at the time, I didn't understand. And that lack of understanding caused me to fail. If I had been in the **WORD,** I would have known not to follow my own heart.

Proverb 3: 5 admonished us: "Trust in the Lord with all thine heart and lean not unto thine own understanding."

But since I would not trust God and His Word, I found myself once again trusting in my fickle emotions and making this foolish promise: **"If the next man in my life doesn't want God in his, then I'm not going to share my knowledge of God with him."**

Any person in their right mind who loves God would know that I had just said the wrong thing. That statement I had only made was an indictment against me. It showed that I hadn't learned my lesson about dealing with men, and I didn't have a personal love walk with God.

Proverbs18:21 states: "Death and life are in the power of the tongue."

James 3: 16 says, "And the tongue is a fire, a world of iniquity: so is the tongue among our members, that it defiles the whole body."

I Pet. 3:10 reads, "For he that will love life, and see good days, let him refrain his tongue from evil, and his lips that they speak no guile."

My idolatrous love for my husbands and loose mouth had separated me from my love for God. During my many years of struggling to maintain a marriage.

It was now apparent that I didn't love my Heavenly Father or my Lord and Savior Jesus Christ, as **HE** desired me to.

I was so messed-up and obsessed by what I had seen of men in the church; that gradually, a lie was birthed in me, and it was this: *Worldly men could give me just as good of a chance of finding a happy and profitable relationship as men in the church.*

All I needed was just a good man, I thought. A foolish idea that had been keeping me in trouble and dragging me, hopelessly, from the **marriage altar** to the **divorce court**.

I will give Jerry this; he was a decent and a good man. But what I still hadn't learned was that just because a man was good didn't mean that he was right for me.

Before my seventh marriage, I had learned that only God could give me the man that was for me. With Jerry, I thought that God had. There were many questions in me. Was it God that brought this man into my life? I was hurt and confused.

Only God knew who he had created for me when He created me. *Had God formed a man for me, and would he eventually bring him into my life?* That was the question I should have been patiently asking.

At this pivotal point in my life, I hadn't asked that question. Therefore, no answer came from the LORD. In fact, at that time, I was so far from God; I was oblivious and confused and bent on self-destruction. If God spoke to me (and I'm sure He was trying), sin had clogged my spiritual ears, and I could not hear.

After my separation from Jerry, I was at a point that was worse than any I had been before. I was about to be overtaken by anger and revenge. My ordeal with Jerry had pushed me to the edge of the cliff. There I stood perilously on edge.

It was, now, the first weekend of my separation from Jerry. We still talked to each other every day. However, he showed little interest in us reconciling and getting back together. I was invited by the ladies I'd been out with two weeks earlier to return to the casino. A sister of one of the girls was in town. They were taking her out to eat and to have a good time.

I was very excited about another opportunity to relax and forget about what was going on in my life.

It would be another girl's night out, and I needed something to help restore some of the damage my womanhood had suffered during the many years I had been with Jerry.

I still couldn't see or realize that my heart was growing *harder and harder*. Not just against my husband, but also God. Little did I realize, this night out with the girls was about to take me even farther from God and deeper into sin.

I would now get an opportunity, just as I had spoken and reasoned in my heart, to meet a new man with whom I would not share my knowledge of God.

The girls and I checked into the hotel early. We later walked around the casino that evening before dinner.

The worldly laughter and discussions among us that afternoon had been a great break from the depressed, mundane, and sheltered life I had been lately living.

It was now time to get dressed for the evening. I waited to dress last; I was in no hurry. I felt great even though I couldn't let go of the idea that I was losing my husband in the back of my mind. Then I consoled myself with this thought: *Let the truth be told, I lost the person-years ago.*

After a few hours, only two of us were left in the room to dress. So we took our time. All suddenly, it hit me. Out loud, the thought in my mind came out of my mouth, "I wonder if that little man I met the last time we were here would be downstairs again tonight?" (I hadn't intended to say this out loud.) A voice came out from the bathroom saying, "You better not go looking for a man; you're a married woman." (She wasn't aware of what was going on with Jerry and me.)

"Jerry doesn't want me anymore," I replied. Then I said, "These people come in and out of these casinos from all over the country,"

I answered back: "He was probably just passing through, just like I was."

"Joann, don't you take yourself down there looking for no man," my friend warned me.

"I'm not." I asserted. Then I thought to myself: *It would be kind of nice to get a little attention again like I did when I was here before.*

"And besides," I thought to myself, "God knows that 'thing' I've been living with as a husband for these past years didn't love or care about me." Finally, we both got dressed, so downstairs we went. As we entered the casino gaming area, the place was packed. The band was playing loud again. The bar area was full.

I heard my girlfriend's words come from somewhere around me, "You better be good."

"Girl, you know me better than that," I shouted into the crowded atmosphere.

I was back at the place I had enjoyed so much two weeks earlier. My thoughts were, now that *I'm here, where am I going to get a seat in this packed-out place?*

The band was a different group than the one from the last time I was there. After listening to the musicians and judging their talent, a thought came to me about the band: Ah, they're alright.

Even though I was still raging inside and troubled about my marriage situation, I was glad to be back at that bar. Something inside of me said, *Let it go and enjoy the night.* So I did.

Standing along the wall area, I began to think: *How will I get a seat around the bar again?*

I was hoping to get in the groove with the musicians, as I had done two weeks ago.

Everyone had a glass or a bottle in their hand. You had to talk loud even though the person was right next to you to be heard. And this guy right next to me did just that. "They are playing good tonight, aren't they?" he asked.

I guess he could see my appreciation for good music as my body motions moved in tune with the band.

I looked at him and nodded my head, confirming that I did. "Like good music, huh?" he continued to drum up a conversation. "Yes," was my answer again, with another nod of the head. He started telling me about how he played different instruments, but mainly in the church.

Now he was talking about something relatable to me.

"What church?"

I asked. "Different ones throughout the city," he answered.

He stopped and took a good look at me. Then with a kind of loud tone, he said, "You're a church girl, aren't you."

"Do I stick out like that," I asked. Instead of giving me an answer, the man instead turned to the other side and started to talk to somebody in a British accent.

As I turned to see who he was talking to, I surprisingly noticed that it was the small-framed man I had met in this bar two weeks earlier.

Then he included me in his British-tone role playing-game between him and the small frame man by introducing this man as his father to me.

They kept the fake British thing up while I tried to go back to focusing on the band.

All of a sudden, the guy at the bar stopped speaking in his British dialect and said, "Oh! My bad." He got up out of his seat and asked me if I wanted to sit. I thanked him for the seat. The small-framed guy then moved closer to the guy playing his son's role, who was now standing; after giving me his seat. They immediately went back to their British roles.

I sat back, relaxed, and once again got back into the music and the band.

The guy who had given me his seat was now involving me in the British role-playing game the two of them had been playing. He turned to me and began to inform me that his father knew good music in a British tone and *all one needed to know about a good drink.*

I wasn't interested, but since he had given me his seat, I felt like I should at least keep acting as I cared about the conversation. The truth was: *I was just grateful to get off my feet.*

I now noticed that even the bartenders behind the bar spoke to this older, framed guy in this fake British accent. Everyone around the bar seems to know him. He was just as loud and happy with everyone as he had been that Friday night two weeks ago. (Guess he wasn't just some guy passing through, huh?) They played the game a little longer, but I found myself thinking about this guy in the same way I did two weeks ago.

Why was this guy so happy? "Loud and happy...." I thought to myself.

"What makes this guy so happy? As a matter of fact, why do all these people appear to be happy out here in the world?"

I had been living a miserable life these last four years with my husband in the church.

"What gives them the right to be so happy?" To be honest, I found myself a little offended about the joy these people seemed to have.

Psalm 37: 1 read, *"Fret not thyself because of evildoers, neither be thou envious against the workers of iniquity."*

Once again, the flesh in me said, "LET IT GO." I took a deep breath and agreed, "Right, just let it go, girl, and try to enjoy the night." About that time, the guy who gave me his seat remembered to get back to me and told the guy he was playing the British game with, "Oh yes, meet my friend, the church lady." This small, framed guy once again spoke to me; then, he kissed my hand. I thought once again that he probably does this with all the women he met around this bar.

As the two of them started to discuss the church lady's information about me, I turned and listened.

O.K. now, I got to deal with why a church lady is sitting around the bar, I thought to myself? I thought to myself that

I'm probably going to have to deal with this: 'what am I doing at a casino' thing also.

To my surprise, the conversation didn't go there. The man that gave up his seat to me asked, "What church do you go to?" I answered him, telling him the name of the church. "What do you do there?" he asked while the small-framed guy listened.

I paused for a moment, took another deep breath, and answered, *I am a minister.*

Then the small-framed guy stepped back, put one hand under his chin and the other on his waist, and asked, "What happened so bad that it has run you out into a place like this?" I looked at him in amazement, wondering why he had asked me this question.

"Something or someone must have done something horrible to cause you to get out of the water?" He added. (Remember I said that I had felt like a fish out of water my first night there, at the bar, two weeks earlier. Now it appeared that this man could see it.) I thought to myself, *how could this guy notice that about me? How?*

I sat there, still a bit spellbound at the moment, thinking to myself, *now just what game is this man going to play with me?*

Before I could come up with an answer, he came with his next comment: "Whatever it was, *just ran you right up in here to me,* didn't it?" At that point, I realized he didn't remember me from two weeks ago. I hadn't forgotten him, but I had forgotten his name.

I didn't answer him, but we kept looking at each other, **eye-to-eye.**

Matthew 6:22-23: *"The light of the body is the eye: if therefore thine eye be single, thy whole body shall be full of light. But if thine eye is evil, thy whole body shall be full of darkness. If therefore the light that is in thee be darkness, how great is that darkness!"*

The anger I had at that time for my husband scares me. As I recall this portion of the story, I now realize that I had allowed the offense to possess me to the degree that I could not see. But looking back, *I can now see that not only was this man at the bar full of darkness, but so was I.*

The anger I had against my husband created darkness in me. Darkness so great; I was considering going to bed with a stranger.

I wish I hadn't kept that eye-to-eye contact with him.

As I listened, this man told me more and more about myself. He was very knowledgeable about church people and the many things they do and say.

I would not know until later that he had dated a female minister right before meeting me. I couldn't take my eyes off of him. Not because of his looks or because I was such attraction to him. It was only because this loud happy-drinking man was telling me about myself. He was not wrong about nothing so far that came of his mouth about me.

Remember when I described myself as a "fish out of water." Well, I was just that. This man now had my attention to keep it for the next eight months of my life. The guy who gave me his seat tried to get back into our conversation, but now, it was not happening.

Finally, he said to the small-framed guy, "Man, I'll see you later."

The guy then turned to me and said, "I can see that you are for sure more interested in my dad, and you're no longer paying me any attention." I was never really paying him any attention. I was just trying to be nice because he gave me his seat.

But he was right about my attention being on his *so-called dad.* How could it not, when this man seemed to see right through me?

"Who ran you out here?" He repeated. I still didn't answer. He looked at me and smiled. Then I asked my question: "You don't remember me, do you?"

He took another drink from his glass and looked at me again. "No," he answers. "Two weeks ago, I met you at this bar," I went on to say. "You were with one of your friends. He gave me his card and talked to me about his business booking cruises", I said.

He took another look at me and still didn't remember me. I went on to point at the bar I was two weeks ago and reminded him how everyone appeared to know I wasn't a regular at the bar.

I began to tell him how I had introduced my girlfriends to him and the cruise guy. I reminded him that as my girlfriends and I left the bar for dinner, he had kissed my hand before I walked away, the same way he had done tonight.

It appeared that the light bulb in his head now came on, and he remembered me. "Did you come looking for me?" he asked again? "No, I didn't," I speedily answered him.

"Yeah, yeah, you came looking for me." "No," I smiled, "I didn't."

I went on to tell him that a chance to come out with my girls was offered, and I took the offer. "No, No," he said, "You came looking for me." Immediately, I begin to question myself. *Had I? I was no longer sure.* Something about this man confused me yet made me interested in him at the same time. He stood back, took another look at me, and asked, "A minister, huh?"

I answered, "Yes, I am," with a bit of an attitude. "What's going on in a minister's life to cause her to come back into my world looking for me?" I didn't respond to that remark. "You're married," he asked?

I answered slowly, not knowing should I answer him or not:

"Yes."

Then with excitement, he said to me: "Your husband… it's your husband who ran you out here, to me." "Well," he said, "*I be damned*. He ran you right into my arms, didn't he? You came looking for me," he told…but not as a question; it was more like a revelation when he made the statement this time.

Before I could respond, he spoke again, but not before he ordered another drink.

"What are you drinking?" "Coke," I answered, and he ordered one, along with his next drink.

Then he got back into our conversation. "It was your husband, wasn't it?"

Why would you say that, I asked? "It would take something awful powerful in your life to push a woman like you out here," he remarked.

"How can you say that about me? You don't know me", I replied.

"You surprise what I know," he said. He was right. Numerous times, during the coming months, we were entangled in this illicit relationship; I would be more than surprised and flattered by his discernment and knowledge.

I was blown away by the people, places, and things this man knew. So often, as we talked during those months, I found myself wondering how a man as knowledgeable about so many things in life as he was would not have a spiritual relationship with God. But I remembered that I had promised myself not to share or push my belief and love for God (which was now fading) on another man.

That night in that crowded bar, it seemed as though we were alone as we talked. It was easy to talk to him for some reason. As we talked, he would reveal more and more of what appeared to be revelations about me.

When we got to the subject of *my many marriages*, he took another drink from his glass, looked at me, and said: "I be damned."

I thought to myself, what revelation is he getting about me now?

"You mean you've been married seven times, and not once did you get a *husband?*" He reflected ponderously.

I sat there in amazement. "How is this man doing this?" I wanted to ask, "How do you do that?"

My grandchildren listened to the song "How do you do that?" by some young lady with pink hair, which would have been right on time.

I knew I was in trouble. Anytime a total stranger can read you that well, it is either God or its demonic I should have been running to get away from that man.

This man had told me more about myself in one conversation than Jerry knew about me after four years of marriage.

Was it true? The things this stranger was telling me.

It may not have been, but at the time, it felt like it and looked like it was mesmerized and enchanted.

I had never met someone so interesting. The night went on, and the two of us continued to talk. We were being interrupted by what seemed like everyone in the bar, women, as well as men. Even the band would call out this man's name from the stage as they played. It appeared that everyone around us knew this guy. And like-wise, he seemed to know everyone. We finally got around to talking about him. I was relieved to talk about him for a change.

Before my girlfriends showed up to pull me away from him to dinner, we exchanged phone numbers.

After dinner with the girls, I was ready to get some sleep. The experience with this man who had looked right into my life and summed it up in such a short time had left me exhausted. I thought Jerry had taken all the overwhelming emotions I had out of me. This man either found more in me or created some more as he talked with me that night.

I was asked question after question, from my girlfriends, about this strange man. I was told again by the same girlfriend who had admonished me earlier: "You better not mess with that man again."

"I'm not," I said.

But time would prove me to be a liar. Everything about this man made me want to know more about him. I would soon be getting the opportunity to experience as we became more intimately acquainted in the following months.

FACING THE RIGHT – CHOOSING THE WRONG

I was alone in the room. The other girls didn't come back to the room right away. I was relieved that I had a few minutes alone. My emotions were confused about what had happened that night at the bar.

Who was this man?

I had had a conversation with someone that both frightened me and aroused me at the same time. My experience with him wasn't like it had been with any other man.

I sat in the room looking at this man's number, battling inside of myself with just what I should do with it. I remembered how Jerry laughed at me when I suggested to him my thoughts about getting some other man to do what he wouldn't do for me. I also remembered what my other male "friend" (who I had almost been sexually intimate with) would always say to me about Jerry.

He warned me that since Jerry had allowed his actions to take the marriage to the point where he cared so little for his wife's needs, he would most likely never change.

And something within me knew that I would be soon facing Jerry, my seventh husband, the same thing I had with every other man I had married -- **the divorce court.**

God forbid if I would have to hear another story from one of my exes about how I was why their new woman was getting better treatment from them than what I had acquired; as if that was supposed to make me feel better and give me a sense of purpose.

Supposedly, they had learned by mistreating me how to treat their next woman. I did not feel better after this revelation. My pain had decreased my self-assurance and confidence as a woman.

"No man will ever love you," the woman who raised my voice still would loudly echo in my spirit.

It does no woman any good to be treated the way I was treated. It was as if he thought he deserved a pat on the back for his newfound self, all at my expense. NO CONGRATULATIONS WERE COMING FROM ME.

I thank God that I have now forgiven my ex-husbands for their mistreatment of me and that I have also allowed God's love to cause me to forgive myself.

My ex-husbands' r*evelation* of believing that they were now much better men with women because of their failed relationship with me wasn't an accurate view and not based on reality.

I may be wrong, even now, for how I view this issue. But my view is this: **Treating a new woman better does not mean that the man suddenly became some great guy since that new woman wasn't the one mistreated by the man in the first place.**

I understand that a new woman will fill a man's head with pride and a lot of praise about himself; most of the time, the woman is glad just to have a man in her life.

He might be *all that* to her now since they have only spent a little time together. But when hard times and disagreements arrive (and they will), this initial *courtship euphoria* will quickly fade away.

"Everything always is good or better in the beginning" is a statement Jerry made during one of the few times he tried to reason with me about why his treatment of me had changed...*Of course, at first, a new woman will always see her new man as being great.* It's because that man hadn't done anything to hurt her emotionally or mentally yet. It is only natural for her to put the woman down, whom the man had mistreated and abandoned. And criticize the woman for not staying around and putting up with **such a great man**, as he (through her infatuated eyes) seemed to now be.

As soon as this new man does the new woman wrong in any way, she's going to expect him to stop treating her that way too. Yet, this new woman will keep putting the woman down that the man was with before her; to make the man feel better about being with her.

Just how many women will send their new man back to the woman they have stolen him from, encouraging him to try giving that woman all the kindness and love that he seemed now to be giving her?

There are a few things that no man or his new woman has the right ever to do: *Ridiculing the mistreated and abandoned woman should be off-limits for them both.*

The Word of God gives instructions about what a person should do when they have <u>an ought </u>or a <u>problem</u> with another.

If you have mistreated me, you better believe I got a problem against you and with you. *"Therefore, if thou bring thy gift to the altar, and there remembered that thy brother has an ought against thee; leave there thy gift before the altar and go thy way; first be reconciled to thy brother, and then come and offer thy gift."* **(Matthew 5:23, 24)**

Reconcile your problem with the person you have wronged or have offended. Don't criticize the person you have wronged to another person to make yourself look good.

When you apologize to the person you have wronged in some form or way, you can then go to God and take your gift to the altar. God will now honor and accept your donation, and HE will hear and answer your prayer.

No one can accomplish any significant growth until they can do right to those they have wronged and ask for forgiveness.

If any one of my husbands had done right about me and had admitted wronging me, I would have patted him on the back in **Jesus's name**. And God would have also been pleased with the man, according to the Word.

The struggle that I was about to take on had nothing to do with God being pleased with me.

It now amazes me; how I could use **God's word** to feed that root of bitterness and anger that was in me, but nothing can justify me (especially the **Word of God**) for doing what I was about to do.

I was finally fed up with what men had done to me and were ready to fight back *my way. Not God's way.*

I was fed up and was now acting as if Jesus was the one to blame for the treatment I had gotten. I sat there that night as a fire-breathing dragon, ready to destroy this man I loved and who had failed me as a husband.

Memories were over-flooding my mind, and for once, I had to face a question that I often suppressed to be able to go on after being hurt by men: **What had all my labors profited me? What had I accomplished?**

I Corinthians 3:13 reads, *"Every man's work shall be made manifest; for the day shall declare it, because it shall be revealed by fire; and the fire shall try every man's work of what sort it is.* I **Corinthians 3:15a** reads, "If any man's work is burned, he shall suffer loss."

My anger with the men who had promised to love me until death departed us and had lied and deceived me-- caused me to plunge within myself, to a new low to a place I had never been.

I had always tried to find good in all my life experiences, whether the experience was good or bad. This time there was no good; I could find only vengeance! ***Just vengeance and retaliation!***

All that Jerry had done to me was wrong. And all of the other husbands had wronged me. **I was angry!**

If Jerry had worked with me, I would never have been here in this room struggling with whether I would keep being faithful to him.

It was his fault, I rationalized. (By reading this, you can tell my mind was on Jerry, not Jesus).

My male friend was right; I sat there thinking. It was only because of how my husband had treated me all these years that I was here at a bar listening to a stranger tell me things about myself; my husband was unavailable for such conversations.

Jerry had cruelly and very rudely abused me, both mentally and sexually. It was his rude way of using me that made me feel I had no other choice. The crazy point was that even at this last moment, before I would sink deeper into captivity, I was thinking about my love for my husband, who hadn't shown me any genuine love for over three and a half years.

Did I go looking for this man? Was it because of Jerry's anger and disappointment that I was seeking and accepting affection and attention from this stranger?

It couldn't have been just for the attention because another man (my male friend) had been there for months showing me compassion, understanding, and more than willing and eager to provide the sex Jerry wouldn't give?

Why? Why this man? And why, why was I having such a hard time doing something to help myself? I must do something different for myself; *I rationalized within my confused and tormented soul.*

(My pain wouldn't allow me at the time, but I wished I would have turned to Jesus in a way that I had never done before and cried out to HIM for deliverance and help).

I started talking to God again, in my mind. God, *I know that you're not going to make Jerry do anything that he doesn't have a desire to do. And he's still showing no desire to do right by me, even after I've moved out and left him.*

"Lord, I have to think of myself," I reasoned within. I was between a rock and a hard place, yet it wasn't easy for me to think only of myself. I didn't use to doing that. I didn't know how.

I was so nervous. Something in me said, "Why make so much out of it... It's just a phone call."

(Not for Joann...it wasn't just a phone call, for me).

All I believed in morally, I would soon forsake. Because of the accumulation of my bad choices, I was about to make another foolish decision that would bring me more misuse and abuse by men; and separate me even further from the God I claimed to love.

I couldn't get myself together. I started to cry, then I thought to myself: *You can't fall apart now, Joann. If your girlfriends come into the room and catch you balling your eyes out, they would have so many questions, and you'll be totally exposed and probably even prevented from finally doing something for yourself.*

I rapidly hit the button on my phone and made the call, rubbing the pain in my right breast, waiting for the phone to ring.

When the phone rang, I wanted just to hang up. Something inside of me began to speak. *What are you doing, Joann?*

My heart seemed to send that question up to my brain. But I had no answer. I didn't know what I was doing; I just felt that I had to do something different this time.

The next question that came up out of my heart was, *what are you supposed to say to this man if he does answer the phone? Even worse, Joann, you are not looking at the fact of what calling this man this time of night is going to say about you, as a person, to him?* At that point, I was even more confused, and I felt lost.

God, how do I deal with where I am again; that was my next question. I can't allow myself to be used by yet another man.

Just as I was about to hang up and breathe for relief, a voice said, "Hello."

My God, I inwardly panted. (It seemed that I couldn't stop calling on God). "Hello," the voice repeated.

"Hi," I replied, as the voice on the phone, very excitedly and joyfully, started talking to me.

Then he asked, "How do you and your girls like the room at the hotel?"

In my mind, the thought came: *That's right. I did tell him we were staying tonight in the hotel.*

I told the man on the phone I loved the hotel, but I wasn't sure about how my girlfriends felt about it. But it was as great as they had expected it to be, I assumed.

He told me it was kind of late and that he had to work the next day. I thought in my mind. "Thank God that one of us knows how to end this call." I very nervously thanked him for an interesting night. "Have a great day tomorrow," I added. He told me that I could call him at work, if I liked, and gave me his work phone number. "You and your girls have a great time tomorrow," he said, and we both hung up the phones.

I was so nervous I had to rush to the bathroom after I got off the phone. My nervousness made me sick to my stomach. I was making myself sick with the place I could see myself going. I had no experience and didn't know what I needed <u>*to do*</u> or <u>*be*</u> now.

I kept talking to God. I was so out of my mind; I didn't know what else to do. (Looking back, I did know what to do: **I should have been praying, <u>*listening*</u> to God, and seeking a way of escape).**

It wasn't like I thought God was going to be a part of my sinful choices. It was just; I didn't know what I was doing, and that frightened me. In my mind, I couldn't stop talking to God. The Holy Spirit was trying to help me, but I would not allow HIM to.

Two different mindsets were going on inside of me. One from what was in my heart and the other from the pain Jerry had caused in my flesh.

Matthew 6: 24 reads, *"No man can serve two masters: for either he will hate the one, and love the others; or else he will hold to the one, and despise the other. Ye cannot serve God and mammon."*

Years of hurt and neglect had me yielding only to my flesh. I was beyond the emotion of hurt. In my mind, I was now delusional over the loss of the man I loved so much. I wasn't in my right mind. And for the next eight months of my life, I would be selfishly thinking only of myself.

Then this question came into my mind; *Joann, several men in your life, had done the same thing to you which Jerry has now done. Why are you reacting this way now?* But I had no answers, only more questions.

Why, *why just being me wasn't good enough for these men? Straighten yourself up, Joann, and fly right;* my brain admonished me.

Then these thoughts rushed in: *Why are you panting so? You can do this.* **Remember?** *You're using it to show your girlfriends how to approach a man they have an interest in. Yes, that's true; I was thinking, but that was years ago.*

Then I started to talk to Jesus again in my mind. *All right, I admit that I married for a lot of crazy reasons before I met and married Jerry. I also acknowledge that many times in my life, I've allowed myself to follow the advice of a lot of people who didn't even have the depth I had. I followed lousy* advice. **Psalms 1:1** reads, *"Walk not in the way of the ungodly, neither sits in the seat of the scornful."*

I continued talking to God. Lord, *I agree that I have been ungodly in all of my marriages by getting sexually involved before I married. I also confess that I was guilty of fornication with every one of them, but I upheld my convictions.*

My motto was this*: If you sleep with me, you marry me;* this was my how-to-stay-saved plan.

Isaiah 64: 6 informs us, *"But we are all as an unclean thing, and all our righteousness is as filthy rags."* I still didn't realize that my **how-to stay saved plan** was my righteousness plan, not the righteousness plan provided by Jesus Christ's death on the cross.

I kept talking to God: *And God, I gave my all to each of these men trying to be what you taught me in your word to be for them. God, even those I didn't love, I was willing to stay with until death departed us, just to get to the place where I could be free from condemnation and at peace with* **YOU.**

I went on: *I let people talk me into a lot of ungodly things with men, from leaving my children's father, which I never really wanted to do--to marrying men that had money and were willing to spend it on me, my family and friends.*

I know I've done wrong, God. I sat there and kept talking to God. *I know now that allowing myself to marry for all these wrong reasons, and listening to others, who talked me into some of those marriages, was wrong. But God, I finally learned after all those years of making mistakes; I married Jerry because I loved him. After all, I believed YOU had sent* him to me. God, I didn't go after Jerry or use my feminine wiles to get him; he found me.

Why, why Lord, am I here? I know we reap what we sow in life, but when am I going to reap from some of the good I've done.

Galatians 6: 7 reads, "*Be not deceived; God is not mocked: for whatsoever a man soweth, that shall he also reap.*"

Since I was a little girl, my life has been filled with pain and confusion. When...when is this madness going to stop? "I told you no man would ever love you," Ms. Lee's voice rang loudly within my tormented soul.

"But you are wrong!" the little girl within me screamed out!

You got to be wrong.

God doesn't want me to go through this all my life. This can't be God's will. Lord, even though Jerry and I failed you through sexual sin, I tried.

I really tried.

Why did I feel this uncontrollable desire to prove to Jerry what I didn't have to prove to the husbands before him? **What**, what was it about Jerry that had driven me to this insane place in life?

Lord, I tried all I could with Jerry Lord; this man doesn't want me. He has shown us both over and over for almost four years that he doesn't want me.

I got to do something different, Lord. Being myself doesn't work. It just doesn't work. I've tried, Lord. I don't know what else to do.

Psalms 46:10: *"Be still and know that I am God."* would have been great right about then. But

I was so angry my spirit couldn't hear anything from God. This time I felt I had to do something different. (I wish that would have meant something Godly and spiritual, but sadly it didn't). I was about to make a move in my flesh and lean to my understanding.

I prayed so God would know that it wasn't because I hadn't tried it HIS way... *(This was my silly thought)*. Sadly, to say, I was thinking, even God couldn't, at that point, give me someone who loved me. **(Ms. Lee had been right.)** And from that moment on, I wouldn't ask God to.

It was time now to take whatever cards had been dealt with me and play my hand. "Win or lose. It doesn't matter," I thought.

It was as though I could justify to God what I had already started to justify within myself; *Jerry has brought me to this point.*

And it was Jerry that had caused me to settle for this mess and do what I was about to do, I mentally concluded.

When the ladies returned to the room, I was dressed and ready for bed. Of course, the ladies had questions about the man from the bar, but I didn't answer any of them.

They had a few laughs, and we slept.

The following day, everyone was a bit slow getting dressed. We decided to go down to the buffet for breakfast. I really didn't want anything for breakfast, so I hung around the room as the others went down to the cafeteria. I had a lot on my mind. One thing was for sure; I wasn't going to allow myself to go back to being that same, Joann. No, **never again.**

What Joann I was going to be, I had no idea. I felt like anything new was better than any of the old Joann I had been.

Satan had been trying to control my mind all of my life and caused me to play the *victim role.* From childhood abuse within the home to my mother's abandonment and many other attacks on my life.

While many people I knew had grown up with *childhood,* I wasn't allowed this opportunity. I had to raise those under me when I was just a child myself. And the embarrassment of growing up with a household full of drunks seemed to linger with me throughout my life.

Then there was all the suffering I had endured. I had been beaten time after time, as a young woman and mother, by the father of my children.

And I could never seem to get away from enduring the humiliation of working years at a factory with black eyes and busted lips from those beatings I endured. But the worst to me was the mistreatment I had received from church people and pastors.

People thought it was funny and joked about the number of times I had been married.

Now, I was enduring mental and sexual abuse from Jerry, the man I loved. The truth was, I could have gone on and on listing the abuse and misfortunes I had suffered throughout my life; the list seemed endless.

Up to that point, I had been trying to *keep it together* so I could be a help to others. I had been fighting all my life to keep my sanity and a *right mind*. It was with my mind that I once loved being in the presence of my Heavenly Father and Lord Jesus Christ. It was with my mind that I had helped so many other women keep their sanity. I also had used my mind to help lost souls open their hearts to my Lord and Savior, Jesus Christ.

It was in my mind that I had succumbed to the idea of never being loved by a man. And it was in my mind that I couldn't realize that I had closed my spiritual ears to the voice of God. With a lot of help from this new man and so many others, that out-of-order spirit would cause me to finally and be taken over and controlled by a **carnal mindset.**

What I couldn't comprehend that night, as I poured my heart out to God, trying to justify what I was about to do; was this simple fact: **Even in a place of such mental and spiritual instability and moral collapse, Jesus and His paternal love over my life were still at work. (Thank You, JESUS!!!)**

Jerry and I discussed the events of my weekend at the casino the following week. Jerry listened to me in his usual unconcerned and uncaring manner.

I had also been keeping in touch with this new *"friend,"* as the worldly women call them, a few times doing the week. I was still baffled about the entire situation. How would I work out things with Jerry since I allowed this new man access into my life?

You are just talking to this guy; that's no sin, I told myself, even though according to the word of God, my husband Jerry and I was **one***,* and I should not have been allowing another man to come into the mix. Nothing sexual was happening with this guy, but conversations about it came up now and then. The seed of adultery was subtly and cunningly being sown.

The one thing I enjoyed about this man was the fact that this man enjoyed talking about things in life that I wanted and had an interest in. He would speak to me about all kinds of different things: The many different jobs he had done in life; all the many different people he knew; all the things those people knew and the things they had done; the many different spiritual people he knew and what he knew about them; what his childhood was like; where he had lived growing up; his college days; his time on the police force; and what his family was like his first wife and their kids, and what it was like with them; his many different experiences with the women he had had and what his relationships with them were like; and how his last girlfriend had a leadership role in her church, just as I did.

It was clear to me that this man had done all he wanted to do in life.

Now, this man was at a point in his life where he was living just how he wanted to live. That was cool with me because at that stage--I was willing to take whatever life brought me and let the chips fall wherever they may. I really wasn't looking or desiring to change anything in his life. Another full-time man to just run over me was far from my plans.

So just what was I looking for from this man? I guess at that time--nothing more than what he was giving.

I was just living day by day, with no plans or goals. My pain and disappointments with Jerry had me paralyzed. I wasn't aware many times of what was going on around me, neither did I care.

Proverb 29:18 reads, *"Where there is no vision, the people perish: but he that kept the law, happy is he."* I was far from being happy in my life at that time. I had stopped even looking for happiness.

Jerry and I still communicated every day. We were talking more than we had in months. Our sexual relationship had improved also. We found ourselves coming together sexually, more than we had done recently.

But now I had a point to prove, and I was still upset about him allowing me to move out. I wanted to go home, but how could I?

Everything in me was so afraid that he would just go back to being that cruel neglector he had been for over the past three years.

It had been a few months since I had moved out and separated from Jerry. Also, it had been a few months since me talking to my new friend.

I was now moving about from place to place because of my financial situation. Jerry was there helping me each time I moved and made the offer that I could still move back home. (God, through Jerry, was yet offering me a way to escape).

This new intelligent man wouldn't let me forget that Jerry had demonstrated over and over that he didn't love me and *how I would be a fool to believe anything he said now.* I was so confused about which way to go. I could see the nice way that this new man treated me. Those around us could see that this man liked me.

All of my friends who knew of the relationship appeared that this guy really enjoyed my company.

This was something I hadn't had in a while, and to be truthful, I was enjoying the attention and the affair.

It was plain to him that I was still very confused about where I was going in life or what I really wanted.

There were many ways about how my new friend treated people that I didn't like. Yet, it was terrific with how he treated me. He would make unkind comments and statements about things and people; that I didn't know, whether they were *true or not.*

Some things he said and did were hard for me to accept at the time, even though I enjoyed being with him. Many things in life I knew I needed to start looking at differently, yet this was so hard for me to do.

I couldn't help sometimes being the Joann I had said I didn't want to be anymore and bring back some things he had said or done to his attention (questioning his reasoning).

I often had to remind myself that he had been exposed to so many different people and was very aware of the many different things people were capable of doing.

I had to fight within myself to sit back and see things from his reasoning and perspective. After being around him for about four months, I still was uneasy about some things he would say and do to people. I just couldn't get past my lifelong motto of doing to others as I wanted them to do unto me.

I didn't like my new friend's accusatory and critical spirit.

Matthew 7:12 reads, *"Therefore all things whatsoever ye those men would do to you, do ye even so to them."*

It was late October now, and my daughter-in-law had been having a lot of problems with coughing. She and my son lived in Chicago. All her family was there. My son had been there since I had moved back home in 2003. They got married the year after I came back down south. She and my son were attending the same church I spoke about earlier, where the pastor wouldn't give me marital counseling when I had so desperately sought it.

From my understanding, the doctors had run some tests and had found a spot on her left lung. The doctor believed that it was just a touch of pneumonia. They started giving her medication for it. Yet, the coughing she had been doing for some months wasn't getting any better. I had an excellent relationship with my daughter-in-law.

Neither of my daughters attended church as I desired, but my daughter-in-law and my son faithfully attended church and served God. I'm not implying that they were prophets or anything like that, but the two of them were very active in the ministry.

Her mother also attended their church, and I felt blessed to have them in my son's life.

My grandson was about three years old, and he was adorable.

I often would upset my son and daughter-in-law because my grandson could do no wrong in my eyes. Whenever they came to visit us or when Jerry and I would visit them, I could never seem to correct this grandson, as I did with my other grandchildren. I spoiled him.

When I met my daughter-in-law in 2002, it had been more than seven beautiful years in which I had her in my life, and I loved her dearly. My son often complained that I loved her even more than I did him, which wasn't entirely true. I deeply loved all of my children, and I had faithfully dedicated them to God when I first got saved back in 1985.

My most heartfelt prayer for years, being a single parent, was for the Lord to *make my son a good man*, the man of God he had created him to be. I knew that this young woman had played a significant part in my answered prayer.

Unlike other mothers-in-law who I knew would always take their son's side on disputes which would come up in the marriage, I would not.

I was hurt to find out just how much my son believed I always took his wife's side in their marital argument. I only wanted them to know and do what was right and respect and cherish one another.

My son didn't know or understand the many different times I would talk to her about working with him and being wise and tolerant. It seemed that I could easily get her to see about my son, what I couldn't or just wouldn't see about Jerry.

People said I talked about her as if she was my child. And to me, she was.

The coughing she seemed not to be able to get rid of concerned us all very much. Despite all the drama I was having in my life with Jerry, I never stopped being an active mother and grandmother to my children or a mother-in-law to my son's wife.

She and I could and would talk about everything. I even spoke to her about my problems with Jerry and this new man I was involved with. She was concerned about what was happening to Jerry and me. Honestly, everyone in my family was.

Jerry was very successful in only letting me see that insensitive man that refused to treat me with loving respect. My baby daughter loved Jerry, and I was bumping heads with her and others in my family about what I was doing with this new man, **_Mr. Intelligence._**

My relationship with this new man would eventually come out, and I would have to deal more and more about my relationship with this man and Jerry. My family and friends knew I was wrong, but it wouldn't be until months down the road when Jerry got himself totally involved with this new woman that they would realize that Jerry wasn't quite right either.

Up until the point that Jerry revealed his real character, I was the only one in the marriage whom my family saw as wrong and out-of-ordered.

Jerry was only telling his side of the story to his family and me, so I was a monster in everyone's eyes.

There is an old saying that _what happens in the dark will eventually come to light._ Even though it was months and months later, Jerry's real ways finally came out of the dark. It was hard on the whole family dealing with Jerry and my separation.

Even though my baby girl was very clear about losing the only man that had played a father role in her life, others missed Jerry too; among them were my beautiful grandchildren. They called

Jerry "papa," and to each of them, papa was gold. Some of them wouldn't turn loose the idea that "papa" and I should always be together. It was hard for all of them, and that made it even harder for me.

The way my grandchildren and family felt about Jerry was one of the main reasons I had done everything I could to hold on to him.

Not many of them cared to hear or understand why I left him. Jerry and I would eventually talk about what the family was going through, but this wouldn't happen until much further down the road. By then, all Jerry could hear when I tried to talk to him about what my family was feeling about our break-up was me putting him down. All he would allow himself to hear from me was how he was just a failure.

When Jerry did go around the grandchildren, he saw how our separation was hurting them.

Because of all the pain my whole family was going through, I stopped going on my Friday night trips to see Mr. Intelligence. Jerry didn't completely stop seeing this new woman, but we both were spending all the time we could re-thinking and discussing all that had happened to us up until that point.

But some people in my life knew the truth about the way Jerry had and still was treating me. I had a couple of friends who were very concerned about how Jerry had never appeared to love me the way a husband should love his wife.

I was incredibly overwhelmed with all that was going on in my family, personal, and spiritual life. It was all weighing me down to the degree that I could no longer properly function. One question that weighed on my conscience was: could I trust a man who has never put my life's cares *before his own*.

I was so consumed that I had forgotten about the pain in that breast and my doctor's concerns about it. I didn't have the money to go back to the doctor anyway, so I guess I didn't think about it. If only I had then turned to My Heaven father and Lord Jesus Christ for help.

"Then came she and worshipped him, saying Lord, help me."

(Matthew 15:25) *Isaiah 41:10 says, "Fear thou not; for I am with thee: be not dismayed; for I am thy God: I will strengthen thee; yea, I will help thee; yea, I will uphold thee with the right hand of my righteousness." But my anger about my life with Jerry had overcome me and had blinded me from the God who is a very present help in times of trouble.*

In the same *overwhelming way,* I knew I could not trust Jerry. It seems that without really realizing it, I felt as though I couldn't trust God either. I could still see how Jerry, in some ways, was even mistreating me. Instead of feeling threatened by this new woman he was going back and forward to, I was consumed with anger. I wanted Jerry to pay for how he had done me.

There were times I felt like Jerry was showing signs of pulling back from this woman. He talked with me about how she wanted him to be sure things were over between the two of us and how she was concerned that I would get back with him one day.

Out of all the many good things she saw about Jerry, she didn't know about this great man she was trying so hard to impress because he was not the kind of man who would tell the truth about anything that would make him look bad.

And the absolute truth about what happened between the two of us would have made him look bad. Jerry never would go into details when it came to intimate things about himself.

I would often encourage him to testify the whole truth about what God had done in his life when he spoke at church or witnessed to others.

If he did this, I told him, he could start walking as that great man of valor God wanted him to be.

I could envision the help that he could give to other young boys and men *who went from one woman to another*, as he had done most of his adult life. "Give God his true glory about what He has done in your life," I would tell him. As far as I know, up to this point, he has never done this.

Maybe, as I think about it now, the reason Jerry hadn't given a true testimony was that Jerry hadn't changed or been *born again*. People telling him what a good man he was, was one of his greatest highs in life. He loved flattery. He would beam with joy when he would tell me of the good things his new woman would say to him about himself. So the likelihood of Jerry ever telling the truth about what he did to cause me to leave our marriage would, most likely, never occur. If left up to Jerry, this story would not be heard by his new woman or any of those unique people in her life who flattered him with praise and adoration.

FACTS ABOUT MY HUSBAND BECAME CLEARER AS MY SPIRITUAL SIGHT GREW DIMMER

Jerry was the kind of man that liked it when people gave him lots of praise. (I seemed to have a pattern of getting with these types of guys) Being the person whom everyone would always comment about *how good of a man he was* very exhilarating for him. Please don't misunderstand me; everyone likes and needs to be encouraged in some form or fashion, but with Jerry, this is what he lived for.

No one in Jerry's life encouraged and supported him more than I did. He often told me how he could see how I put his needs and wants above my own. And some of my friends felt that I was still doing this.

On those rare occasions when Jerry admitted that he might have been wrong, it never was to the point of him having true repentance or remorse; because he would quickly go back to how he was acting in the first place.

There was no way this new woman was going to see the real Jerry at this time. It would take years before my family and many others would even *see the real Jerry.*

During many of Mr. Intelligence and my conversations, I can remember when he would say that he was looking for Jerry to show up at the bar one of those nights when he and I were meeting together.

He would say that the more he realizes and sees the unique woman I am, the more he knew that Jerry would show up to get me back.

After several months of not seeing Jerry coming to claim what was rightfully his, he could finally discern that there was no way my husband could really love me. That was very much the same thing that my close friends had observed and expressed about Jerry to me.

They would say to me that even though it might be true that Jerry was struggling with the issue of whether he wanted to go forth as this other woman's man totally, it is evident to them that he didn't love or care about me, as his wife.

One of the things about Mr. Intelligence I appreciated was that he was what *he was.* He wasn't going to put on an act for anyone. If he did, it was for his twisted desire, not anyone else. *You get what you see was his attitude.*

This was one of the most frustrating things about him. But since I had been living with

Jerry's hypocrisy for all of those years, this was one of the things I admired about Mr. Intelligence. He was always genuine, even though he could take it too far at times.

Finally, Jerry made an offer which showed me how he felt about me and proved that he didn't love me. He wasn't aware that I wasn't talking to or seeing Mr. Intelligence anymore, so he made me an offer. He told me I could keep seeing this man, get whatever attention I needed, but just come back home.

I was convinced that he wasn't willing to take on the responsibility of taking care of my emotional needs--both now and forever, for the rest of our lives.

I wanted Jerry to be angry with me for what I had done and to tell me he would be the only man giving me the attention I needed for the rest of my life. He didn't have to say it in those exact words. But the offer he made me should have been somewhere along those lines.

When he offered to share me with another man, I became furious and even angrier with him.

I was so caught up in my own emotions I didn't recognize that my husband was turning back to me. So, I foolish stayed in my pride and asked what kind of person do you think I am? Do you really think I could do something like that, I asked him?

Now I didn't know that maybe he was trying to find a reason to leave his girlfriend alone. I also couldn't see that maybe that was the best he had to offer me. That he was trying.

Jerry didn't understand that by him allowing me to see how easily and willingly he could leave this other woman, he was giving me a glimpse, or a preview, of what he would do to me in the future. I didn't realize how out of order my mindset was because he was my husband, and his desire should have been to come back to his wife, leaving that relationship with her.

This would have been the perfect time for both of us to seek God. But neither of us could see it then.

Psalm 37:5 states, "Commit everything you do to the Lord. *Trust him, and he will help you.*" We had gotten so far away from trusting in the Lord; we both found ourselves blindly *stumbling more and more into spiritual **darkness**.*

I only saw Jerry's offer to share me with another man as proof that he was still that same old man who was incapable of giving anything more. There were no signs of a *real change of heart* in Jerry. His offer to share me with another man revealed that his mind hadn't changed or been renewed. I didn't realize that my fears set in my soul from Ms. Lee's confession no man would ever love me was still working in my sub-consent mind.

What was more messed up than Jerry's thinking was my own. We were both totally out of the will of God. As strong as I had once been in the spirit. So why was I expecting any real change in Jerry's heart and mind when neither of us wasn't totally sold out to God in the first place?

Matthew 18:3 reads, "And he said, Verily I say unto you except ye be converted, and become as little children, ye shall not enter into the kingdom of heaven."

I now believe that there was never really a true conversion of Jerry's heart. I'm not God, but I do not think that Jerry was ever born again, even though I had no right to judge him. Even though Jerry was faithful in his church attendance, so was I. I felt that all we were going through caused me to now believe he ever fully surrendered himself to God. Jerry wouldn't allow God to renew his mind. Jerry refused to humble himself as a little child and submit himself to God. I now see that maybe Jerry was doing just that humbling, and I was too angry to acknowledge that fact.

I was more focused on being right. So, I only looked at knowing the Lord had spoken personally to Jerry twice. Once from his pastor, whom he served in the role of a deacon. The pastor told Jerry specific things God wanted him to do. Another time, an Evangelist visiting the same church gave Jerry another prophetic word. She told Jerry that the Lord was showing her how he needed to humble himself. Until this very day, I don't believe Jerry has submitted himself to God. Again, I was so determined to make Jerry the bad guy that I could pray for him but not forgive him. So, I prayed that one day, he'd cry out in repentance to God and become that *great man of valor* I've envisioned him to be. LORD, why could I not realize that he was displacing be that great man of valor even then.

Luke 12:3 reads, "I tell you, Nay: except ye repent, ye shall all likewise perish."

True repentance is when you become so godly sorrowful, and tired of living your life your way that from that moment on, you live life only the way God instructs you to live it in his Word. And you turn away from the wrong you were doing, with the sole intent never to go back to it.

I feel now that what Jerry was saying to me could have been him truly repenting. But since he wasn't doing it my way, I didn't view it as repenting. So, I pushed my husband onto this woman without realizing what I was doing. Now he was dealing with a situation with her that led him to tell me that the reason he could not stop his adulterous relationship with the woman he was involved with was this: "Joann, you just don't know how much hell I'll go through with this woman if I did what you are telling me I need to do, to be right with God."

My response was this instead of being compassionate with him I chose to be religious: "So Jerry, you would rather die and go to an eternal Hell than to experience the temporary hell this woman would give you on earth?

Proverbs 6:26 reads, "for by means of a whorish woman a man is brought to a piece of bread: and the adulteress will hunt for the precious life."

"But you just don't understand," he replied." "No, I understand more than you will ever know about the price and pain one goes through when one has to give up something or someone, they want to stay in right standing with God…

Remember", I asked Jerry, "You force me to have to give you up."

John 3:3 reads, *"Jesus answered and said unto him, except a man be born of water and the Spirit, he cannot see the kingdom of God."* Jerry did go down into the water when he joined the church back in 2004. So, he did experience a form of water baptism. I realize that baptism with water does not save a person, but we, as the people of God, are baptized because we believe in the death, burial, and resurrection of Christ.

Baptism represents a believer's death and resurrection; it symbolizes a believer being washed, cleansed, and made a new *creature or creation* in Christ.

When a person repents of their sin and converts to faith in Christ, that person in obedience to

God's Word they often are water baptized. Water baptism doesn't save a person, but it is what a believer does to represent that he or *she has been born again into Christ Jesus.*

When we accept Christ as our Lord and Savior, we are instantly born of the Spirit of God. Our **spirit-man** is made new, but our **body** and **soul**, which comprises the *mind, will,* and *emotions,* may not be changed in that exact moment. Therefore, the believer must consistently work on renewing his or her mind through the Word of God.

My disappointment in what my husband was carrying thought made me personally not believe he was ever born again or saved, but I am not God to know for sure.

Jesus says in **John 3:6**, *"That which is born of the flesh is flesh; and that which is born of the Spirit is spirit."* To be saved, one must be born of the Spirit of God.

How could I have been expecting something different in Jerry's thinking when I knew it took that consistent through the teaching of the word of God? Here I was born of the spirit and filled with the Holy Ghost since 1985 and look how messed-up my actions still were from the evils and dysfunctions I had endured throughout my life.

In **Romans 12**, the Word teaches us as believers; *to be not conformed to this world but to be transformed by the renewing of our mind.* Therefore, a person can be born again, but if that individual does not allow him or herself to grow by renewing their mind with God's Word, they can sometimes act like the *sinners in this world*.

I Corinthians 2:13b-15 reads, "...But which the Holy Ghost teaches, comparing spiritual things with spiritual. But the natural man receives not the things of the Spirit of God: for they are foolishness unto him: neither can he know them, because they are spiritually discerned. But he that is spiritual judged all things, yet he himself is judged of no man."

You can see and understand why I couldn't judge those things about Jerry back then.

Operating in the flesh from a carnal mindset, I wasn't spiritually capable of even discerning my spiritual condition. I was so far out of God's will for my life.

I was expecting Jerry to have what he needed for me naturally and say to me what could only truly come from a spirit-filled man, a spiritually-minded man who was allowing the Spirit of God to teach, guide, and lead him into **all truth.**

Christian women, please listen. Let us stop getting invoked with an **unsaved man** and then praying for God to save him and sanctify him just because now we have him. Let us accept the responsibility that comes with our decision to get with any man we involve ourselves with. The **Word of God** teaches us not to be unequally yoked together with an unbeliever. Pray for the man that the LORD would do the converting needed in his soul and stop trying doing it ourselves.

Proverbs 12: 15 reads, "The way of a fool is right in his own eyes, but he that hearkens unto counsel is wise."

John 3:7 reads, "Marvel not that I said unto thee, Ye must be born again."

Neither my husband nor I were really trying to understand the ***things of God's kingdom***, which Christ has made available for His people *here on earth*. As I look back now, maybe we were trying, and that was why we were talking to each other than about our outside relationship we had gotten ourselves into, and the devil didn't want us to realize we were.

Matthew 4-17 reads, "And from that time Jesus began to preach, and to say, repent for the kingdom of heaven is at hand."

As a believer, I now understand that one must have a **kingdom mindset** in all matters concerning our life here on earth. At that time, my perspective centered on my man and my family hindered mine.

John 1:5 states, "And the light shineth in darkness; and the darkness comprehended it not."

I wanted my husband to comprehend the light I was desperately reaching for in him when clearly, he was in darkness and without the spiritual Light of Christ, but so was myself. I had so much anger in me; I was in a deep place of darkness myself. Sadly, to say, but for a long time, being so wrapped up with my marital problems, I became spiritually blind in that matter of my heart. Coming from my background, I could I not?

My husband's double-mines continue. He would do right for a while, and then he would go back to that *I don't give-a-darn attitude.*

In my mind, I had wasted over three and a half years trying to keep Jerry in my life. But I still found myself wanting to believe in his promises *that he had changed* and that he now recognized and could see the wrong he had done to me.

Being Joann, I couldn't leave good enough alone. Since you have now changed Jerry, please answer this question: Why are you still treating me so cruel?

Being Jerry, he dropped his head and answered, "I don't know." "You don't know!" I yell, *losing it again.*

"How in the hell can you treat someone as bad as you have treated me and tell them you don't know…Why? Why? Why? Why were you so cruelling to me for all of those years?" I started to fall apart again, and I cried.

Jerry answered again, looking up at me,

"Joann, I don't know. Maybe there's something wrong with me. I just don't see or feel about love the way you feel about it. I don't think I've ever understood it to be what you are saying it should be. I don't remember ever feeling with any woman I've ever had the way you talked about how it should be. I don't even feel this for this woman. I keep telling you that *no woman has ever required of me the things you do.*"

"And to be honest," he said, "I've done more things for you than I ever remember doing for any other woman in my life. I have never had trouble getting a woman, so when my relationship with one doesn't work, I move on to the next. There have always been one or more women available for me to move on to. I'm telling you the truth. I really don't know why I treat you or have treated you the way I have."

I thought in my mind: If he doesn't know why he mentally and sexually abused me for all those years, how am I supposed to see if I can trust anything he's saying now.

From what Jerry had just told me, he could revert to his neglectful self at any time. He had given me no assurance. What was there for me to believe in, except fear?

I wanted to believe in my husband and go back to my marriage, but I was scared. I was too afraid to trust him; and too hurt and angry with Jerry to believe anything from him. After listening to Jerry, I didn't know what to do.

I can see now I was allowing my fears that originate from what Ms. Lee implanted in my life made it easy to believe he would never love me right instead of trusting God that we both were a new creature in Christ Jesus. So, I foolish stay away from my husband. Allowing him to get more and more involved with this new woman as time went on. She had started introducing him as her man he told me to her family and friends.

The clearer I saw Jerry, the more I could look back and see the differences between him and Mr. Intelligence. I often found myself thinking about the differences in them. I couldn't help but compare them. Mr. Intelligence had introduced so many new things into my life.

I learned a lot of new information from Mr. Intelligence about many things I had never opened myself up to before. Even though I didn't tell my husband, I did pull back from him. I had stopped going around him completed. It was easy to assume he was out of my life for good because of how he had told me that once a woman walked away from him, he never took her back. I could remember testimonies he had shared with me about women who had walked out of his life.

I recalled all the things he told me he had done to them and how he treated them once they left him. As I talked with my friends about him, I relayed to them how I didn't feel I could get this man to understand all the things that were going on in my head, *as if he would want to try to understand my world anyway.*

He had expressed how important my children, grandchildren, and my being a mother-in-law were to me. That was one of the many things he always brought to my attention and insisted he admired about me.

He would often joke about how he was going to move me away from them. He felt that he would never truly have me to himself because of the love and determination I had for my family. He also could see that I was still in love with my husband. My thoughts jumped from Jerry and Mr. Intelligence during that time, causing me to ponder about the difference between them.

Two things bothered me about going back to my husband. Firstly, I couldn't get that scene out of my head how he had laughed at me when I asked him for help to fight those thoughts, I were about to allow someone else to do what he wouldn't do in the bedroom. Maybe it was that indignation that had me with this man in the first place. Was I veganity trying to prove a point to my husband? Secondly, it was consistently bothered me was his answer that *he didn't know why he had treated me the way he had for all those years.*

Now that my husband was aware that I had gotten involved with Mr. Intelligent, and it was over, but Jerry didn't know that his attitude of having sex with me had become <u>anyplace</u> and <u>anywhere</u>.

But now, something had happened to me, and my feelings about sex with Jerry weren't the same. **Something had taken over me.**

Since I left my husband, I had lost a secure place to stay. Jerry kept offering that I could come back home and live with him instead of constantly moving from place to place. But my pride and fear would not allow me to do this, knowing how he changed so smoothly in his treatments toward me. He had taught me well about what he could be when he wanted to, which I felt was a cold-hearted, low-down dirty dog.

Jerry could show those he wanted to impress one side and those he didn't care for, another side of him. Therefore, I had no idea when I could end up on his wrong side.

He had played his adorable and loving role so well during the first year we were together that I thought God had answered my prayers when he came along.

But the years I spent with Jerry seemed as though Ms. Lee (the child-abuser who raised me) had come back from the dead and lived within him, and this time she had hate for me greater than she had when she was alive.

Jerry as any human capable of lying. I was afraid of being his victim again. The woman who would fight for her marriage had died. I wanted to believe that the woman that loved Jerry also had died, but that just wasn't true. I still was making room for him in my life whenever he needed it.

Even though I thought I wanted to go forward without him, it was as if I couldn't stop fighting him to protect him from himself.

During this time, someone very childish started calling me. This person would harass me about my husband being with this new woman. Her comments would range from this new woman's sexual activities with my husband to her small-minded remarks about how Jerry now belonged to someone else.

The calls persisted for a while before I finally addressed Jerry about them. To be honest, being the type of woman I was, I just looked over the childish behavior of the unidentified lady.

Of course, she had me thinking as anyone would that the calls were coming from Jerry's new woman. However, someone I knew said that it was probably someone familiar with the situation who was either seeing or being told this information in person.

After Jerry confronted his new woman about the calls, she said that it wasn't her. To admit that it was her or even that she knew who it was would show her immaturity and how small-minded she was when she was trying to impress him the most.

Proverbs 5:3-5 says, "For the lips of a strange woman drop as a honeycomb, and her mouth is smoother than oil. But her end is bitter as wormwood, sharp as a two-edged sword. Her feet go down to death; her steps take hold on hell."

After the phone calls wouldn't stop coming to me, Jerry appeared to try to get to the bottom of who was doing the calls. He called me with her on the phone without informing me; this was just a waste of all our time.

As I stated earlier, what woman in her right mind who was trying to keep a man in her bed and life would be woman enough to admit to that man that she was capable of being so smallminded as to take part in playing silly games over a phone.

Nevertheless, since Jerry had given me no warning about the phone call, I couldn't stop him in what I felt was his selfish attempt to play *the good guy role*. Again, she responded the only way any other woman would respond--by saying that it wasn't her making the calls.

Then she added that she was woman enough to tell me anything she wanted me to know to my face. Not realizing that the true meaning of being a ***real woman*** or ***woman enough*** meant to me *not to lower oneself to sleep with another woman's husband* until he's no longer that woman. But the truth was I to have been guilty of what I was so angry with her about.

She had involved herself intimately with my husband. The childish calls continued.

When I was small, I used to hear old people say," Why buy the cow when you can get the milk free?"

Many of us have been that self-centered woman investing all our time and money and allowing a man to move into our home before requiring that his divorce papers had been filed and on the way to court. I know this is because I also had been one of these women.

Jerry's shacking partner then said that it wasn't anyone she knew who was making the harassing calls as far as she knew. But I asked why a woman would take so much interest to torment me when she wasn't the one sleeping with Jerry or at least getting some joy from him; I couldn't understand.

But what I have now seen and learned about what people will do, nothing surprises me anymore.

The more detailed the calls got about what Jerry was doing with this woman, the more it indicated that it had to be someone with the two of them seeing everything that was going on or someone that received the information from one of them first-hand. At that point, I felt that it would be small of me even to allow the calls to bother me.

My family believed that Jerry knew more about the calls than he was admitting. At this time, they finally began to see something different in Jerry- other than what he had shown them; they now saw a different side of him.

I believed Jerry didn't know who was making the calls, but most of my friends thought I was naive or foolish to believe this. He knows something about who's making those calls, they would say. The comment was: *If he doesn't know, his woman knows, or someone around her knows something.*

The people in my life believed what they did because the calls were always giving me more details about what he was doing with her, and when I would confront him, he would admit it was true.

It got to the point that the information given to me about him, and the woman provided me with the truth about specific actions he was doing with her. But there I was - *still giving him the benefit of the doubt.* Because I still loved him. Around that time, I moved in with one of my girlfriends. During the summer months, when I would go to the casino bar to meet with Mr. Intelligence, she often came with me. After moving in with her, we spent a lot of time talking and discussing things.

We had the kind of friendship where she could get right to the point with me about anything. But I also had that same freedom about any subject in her life. She observed how patient I had been with Jerry, even before I moved in with her. It was beginning to anger her, I think, about how much I loved and cared for a man who was mistreating me.

One day, while we were sitting around watching television, she finally spoke up. "I don't see why you just don't let Jerry go, Joann," she said.

She could see I was a **confused mess** and could see how far I had gotten away from God. The odd thing about it, I was staying with her when I first met Jerry. Now, after almost four years of being with Jerry, I was right back where I started *with her.*

When I first met Jerry, she didn't like him. And she told me then that he wasn't the one for me.

She always felt that there was just something about Jerry that wasn't real. She told me back then that she wasn't comfortable with how I had fallen so head-over-heels for him, but I fought with her about him. In a lot of ways, I was still fighting against the opinion she had of him.

She had seen Mr. Intelligence, and she had told me things that she didn't like about him too. She was aware there were some things that I didn't like about Mr. Intelligence also. She had also seen the kind way he treated me when he was around me. I admitted that Mr. Intelligence showed me the kind of care Jerry hadn't shown me in years. With Mr. Intelligence, I was experiencing new things and seeing and meeting new people all the time.

My girlfriend was now wondering the same thing as I was about Jerry: Did I want to go back to a man that could dog me out the way Jerry did when there was someone who appeared to appreciate me?

There were a lot of good things I admired about Mr. Intelligence. One of those things was: during the time I spent with him, he never tried to change me. I didn't attempt to change him either. As for me being a woman of God, he really didn't seem to have any problem with--since during that time of my life, I wasn't living or acting like a woman of God anyway.

Mr. Intelligence had once been married to a woman whose family was a part of a big church, and he had also had an intimate relationship with a woman with a leadership position in the church before he met me. *You do you, and I'll do me was the type of guy Mr. Intelligence was, as long as you are there when I need you.*

He always tried to enlighten me about new things, some of which I didn't understand and didn't want to--or felt was non-sense.

I had two reasons why this didn't bother me about him. First, it was because he was so much more knowledgeable about people, places, and things than I was. He had seen places and experienced some things that I was still dreaming and hoping to see and do in life. The other reason was that; I was still very innocent in my thinking, and this man is enlightening me about people and causing me to see people more for who they were, which was new to me.

In my mind, I was now mixing up the treat people like I wanted to be treated law of God with the; be wise as a serpent, but gentle as a dove scripture.

In Matthew 10:16, Jesus says, "Behold, I send you forth as sheep in the midst of wolves be ye therefore wise as serpents, and harmless as doves."

Mr. Intelligence could see that I was just too trusting when it came to people in general. He could understand and accept natural things far better than he could spiritual things. I thought could *put up* with him much better than I could with Jerry because he was true to himself and not a hypocrite. He hadn't, for a moment, even from our first encounter, pretended to be something he wasn't.

Jerry had consistently lied about who he was. Through our courtship until the day we were married, I believed his lies because I wanted to, even though I felt he was now lying to me about everything.

There were other differences between these two men, which I would bring up in my conversations with people at some point or another.

At times, I would bring up things I didn't like about Mr. Intelligence to him. And in the same fashion, he would voice his opinion of me.

After we discussed our disagreements, we could go on as though nothing had happened. And we wouldn't dwell on what we had said about each other. I had never met anyone that was so comfortable about where they were in life and in their own skin than Mr. Intelligence. He had been to many places and had done many things in life. Now, he was delighted with what seemed to me to be a *very small world*.

I had vowed never to push my beliefs and faith on another man again; his world, which mainly consisted of that casino area, was all right with me.

Now that I'm looking back at it, I had never imagined his world being mine anyway. Somewhere, in me, was still the belief that God had more in life for me. Even with this man in my life, I couldn't let that belief go.

I'm having a hard time keeping myself together as I write this. There are many reasons I'm taking so much time to fill in every tiny detail of my life. During this time, the cancer was present in my body, and I was oblivious to it, for the **invader** had not yet been diagnosed or discovered.

Hopefully, reading about how messed-up and distorted I had allowed the devil to *cloud up my world*, those of you who are reading this will be able to appreciate why: **I Thank God for Cancer!**

True deliverance comes when one truly understands just how bad his or her condition is. I had now realized that my whole life was in turmoil and that spiritual darkness had completely enveloped me. I realized my condition escalated and that I had been in a state of bondage all my life, and despite all the effort I exerted, *It appeared I could not escape.*

Even though life's hurts and disappointments were spinning my life out of control, there was something down inside of me that still believed that God would yet do a great work in me and through me. **Thank God for grace!!!**

There's a song church people sing that says: *Something down inside of me is telling me to go ahead.* Even though *I had and was* neglecting my born-again spirit man, deep inside, the Spirit of God was still interceding for me.

I am amazed at the goodness of God and how much HE loves us and wants to save us so that we can one day dwell eternally with Him in His kingdom. Even as I write this, God reveals things to me, as He encompasses me in His secure and loving arms.

The small amount of food that I was feeding my *spirit man ever so often* kept my spirit alive enough for it to bail me out of my mess and deliver me from my bondage in the future.

I know now that, *therefore* I couldn't stop going to church, even during the deepest and darkest part of my rebellion against God.

During those months, when I was committing adultery, the devil fought me continuously in my mind saying that; it was foolish to keep going to church, yet, by God's grace, I continued going.

Please, please, Heavenly Father! Please, please don't let one reader of this book get the wrong understanding of what I am saying.

God forbid that anyone reading this book get the wrong idea that I'm saying that it is alright to go to the house of God every week and hear the Word of God and continue to commit adultery or any other habitual sin. It is not okay or alright! God is a Holy God. His desire is for us to live our lives in the light, walking in the integrity of His Word and clothed with the righteousness of His Son.

I am saying that if you have fallen into a sinful practice of committing adultery, fornication, or any other sin in the house of God, don't stop going to church. Please keep going and listening to the word of God and pleading at the Altar for deliverance and help.

Keep paying your tithes and offerings to God.

And don't let your weakness, whatever it may be, keep you from God or keep you from believing that Jesus has already overcome **<u>all sin</u>**. And even in your mess (*no matter how deep and messy it is*), **HE** can still get you out.

Even though I was still living in sin, I kept going to church and paying my tithes and telling others of God's goodness and greatness. I just couldn't stop.

There was a fight going on inside me, a battle between my carnal man (flesh) and my *spirit man*. The **Word** I was hearing was feeding my spirit and soul, and I strongly believed the tithes and offerings I was sowing were rebuking the devourer as I continued to partake and sow into the **Kingdom of Light.**

O, my God, it was working! Your Word **LORD** was really working.

II Corinthians 9:10 reads, "Now he that ministered seed to the Sower both minister bread for your food, and multiply your seed sown, **and increase the fruits of your righteousness.**"

THANK YOU, LORD JESUS, FOR THE POWER OF YOUR WORD WORKING IN ME (REGARDLESS OF HOW SMALL I THOUGHT IT WAS IN ME), DURING THOSE DARK DAYS OF MY LIFE!!!!!!

A well-known proverb quoted in some churches is little word, little power; much word, much power; no word, no power.

Even though I felt that God's Word was small in my life because of my sin, the Word was carrying **power** to my soul and spirit as I continued digesting it into my heart.

The word of God was still working in my life, even when I felt as though I had no power or strength.

But that wasn't true; I did have power at work within me, even though I saw it as <u>little</u>. The **Word** of God is quick and powerful and sharper than any two-edged sword, and God has exalted **His Word** even above **His Name**. Heaven and earth shall pass away, but the **Word** shall never fail.

Thank God, I now have the sense to know that I can't live the victorious life God created me to live without staying, always, in the **Word**. The more Word I not only know but understand and speak, the more power I'll have and the more like Jesus I'll become.

For when I speak the **Word**, it's the spirit of Jesus Christ that speaks. I'm just the instruments that Jesus is using when I proclaim his Word. I understand Jesus has *all power*, and I, too, can have *all the energy I need* to accomplish whatever I need in this world when I speak the word *in JESUS' name*. "*So then after the Lord had spoken unto them, he was received up into heaven* *and sat on the right hand of God. And they went forth, and preached everywhere, the Lord working with them, and confirming the <u>**Word**</u> with signs following. Amen."* **(Mark 16: 19, 20)**

Matthew 28:18 says, "All power is given unto me in heaven and in earth."

I have always loved studying and searching for the Word of God. I'm grateful, as I look back over my life for the time I spent diligently searching God's Word. Bible study was now paying off. The Word was still down inside of me. **THANK YOU, JESUS!**

"Thy word have I hid in mine heart, that I might not sin against thee." **(Psalm 119:11)**

I had to be messed up in mind to think that I could be religious and assume that just knowing the **Savior** was enough, even while I was living a carnal life and making fleshly decisions.

I had allowed my pain and disappointment in a man to rob me of my spiritual rights and the benefits of being a royal daughter of the **KING**.

Narrow-minded thinking had driven me from searching and studying God's Word to a **dark place** where I was trusting in another man--even more than I was trusting and believing for my husband Jerry and his deliverance.

At first, I hadn't done anything but talk to Mr. Intelligence. But Jerry didn't believe that. He was aware of my sexual weakness and the fact that he had fallen short in this area for a while, in giving me what I needed.

The long conversations and quality time I spent with this man shortly after we had first met gave Jerry a good reason to believe that we were sexually involved. During those days, I was still trying to pay Jerry back for those years of his sexual neglect of me. So, I talked to this man openly and audibly on the phone, in the presence of Jerry.

Not being sexually involved with Mr. Intelligence was hard for anyone to believe who knew about my sexual addiction. Honestly, it was even a surprise to me that we hadn't gotten sexually involved. Maybe, after all those months of being sexually neglected by Jerry, a change had taken place within me, of which I wasn't aware. Mr. Intelligence and I had been together for almost four months, and we hadn't been sexually involved. This wasn't characteristic of him or me. It wasn't like either of us to have been dating for almost four months without getting sexually intimate. He had let me know that he usually would have dropped a woman that he talked to for so long in which there was no sexual involvement.

When I stopped seeing Mr. Intelligence, I never told him why. But since he had told me he never takes a woman back after leaving him, I felt that the relationship was over with, anyway.

I still hadn't told Jerry that I had stopped seeing Mr. Intelligence even though we talked regularly and about almost everything. For some crazy reason, the two of us would occasionally find ourselves deep in discussions about the **Word of God.**

I say this was crazy because we both had slacked off and had stopped discussing God's Word as a couple.

Now we found ourselves searching the Word almost the way we had done during that year of dating before we were married.

Even though we were studying the bible together, Jerry was, at the same time, getting more and more involved with this new woman in his life. During those days, we both were still attending church services. I wonder now that if I had told him then that I hadn't had sex with Mr. Intelligence, would it have made him leave this woman that he was seeing. Only God knows the answer. (But maybe, just maybe, God was trying to give us a way out). **I Corinthians 10:13** reads, *"There hath no temptation taken you, but such as is common to man: but God is faithful, who will not* *suffer you to be tempted above that ye are able; but will with the temptation also make a way to escape, that ye may be able to bear it."*

There were moments that I would try to enlighten Jerry about how he had treated me, and this would always start an argument and us battling over who was right and who was wrong. It seemed like whatever word we heard when we did go to church was being stolen the moment, we had to deal with our marriage problems.

It looked as if the messages we heard while in our churches were not changing anything in either of us when it came to our marriage.

I was driving to Arkansas, attending my spiritual father's church, and Jerry was still attending the church where we both had participated together, performing his role as deacon.

By attending separate churches, the enemy had another way to pull us apart and push us further and further away from God. I knew Jerry had gone back to some of his worldly ways long before we separated. No matter how he tried to get me to believe that he had changed, I knew that Jerry was still filled with pride and was still living in sin.

Jerry wasn't the man he was trying to make me believe he was, or he pretended to be. My friends didn't think Jerry had changed, and neither did Mr. Intelligence before I abruptly stopped seeing him.

I wanted to believe in my heart that Jerry was experiencing some regrets about our marriage. Yet, I couldn't overlook the things I was seeing him do. I think he was having regular conversations over the phone with his old lover from up north even before he got himself involved with this local woman. I'm just not sure about anything when it comes to the things Jerry was doing.

He often boasted about how he had stayed alone in the house after I had moved out for over eight months before he physically got involved with this new woman. But he never really looked at the fact that he was intimately involved with his old lover up north before his co-worker sister (the lady he now was seeing) made her move on him through phone calls.

Sadly, to say, Jerry and I were engaging in *a tic for-tat* kid's game rather than seeking God for help.

Because I did not wholly seek God, my spiritual view of HIM was fading and was *growing dimmer and dimmer.*

BACK INTO THAT SMALL WORLD

I wasn't treating Jerry like the scripture teaches. **Roman 12:20-21** instructs us, *"Therefore if thine enemy hunger, feed him; if he thirsts, give him drink: for in so doing thou shalt heap coals of fire on his head. Be not overcome of evil, but overcome evil with good."* I was handling Jerry as the worldly man or woman handles a person who can't be trusted. It was clear that I couldn't trust Jerry. Not only was he untrustworthy with me, but he was the type of person who no one could trust.

One morning, my roommate and I were having breakfast, and the trust issue with Jerry came up in our conversation. She was more than aware of all that I was still going through with Jerry, and she was not happy about it.

"It's your life," she said, "but Joann, that man just isn't right when it comes to you." She wasn't telling me anything that I didn't know. I felt foolish, though, because I still had a little hope for reconciliation.

Mr. Intelligence was the next topic, from my girlfriend's mouth, as we sat for breakfast. "Did you ever hear from him again?" "Who?" I asked. "Don't play crazy with me," she responded. "You know who I'm talking about." "No, I don't," I said.

"Why did you say that," she asked?

"You remember I told you he warned me that if a woman left him, she could not come back. Once you leave him, you can never go back."

"Maybe," she said, "but something is going on a little different with you and him, Joann. I don't think that remark included you."

"Don't start!" I got a little loud with her. "Don't get all bent out of shape with me. I just asked", she retorted.

"I've had enough rejection from men," I said, as I reminded her that he had told me about the way he had treated some of the women in his life who had tried to come back to him.

"No, I need to leave him in that little world of his, *down there,* where he is so satisfied," I told my friend. She watched me as I kept rubbing my right breast.

"Is it hurting that bad, Joann?" she asked with concern. "At times," I answered. "What are you doing for the pain?" she continued.

"There's not much I can do until I get back on Jerry's insurance," I told her. She got loud, "See, that's what I'm talking about! How could that no-good Negro forget to put his wife on his insurance policy?"

"Nah! Nah! We won't go there", I replied. "All it will do is just get me *down-hearted again*," I told her.

My girlfriend worked days, and I worked nights. After she went out the door to go to work that morning, I closed the door behind her and told her to have a good day. I thought how irresponsible Jerry was to allow his health insurance coverage on me to drop. But that was my Jerry, the husband that didn't give a damn about his wife. I fought hard to let this thought go to get some rest that day, but it wasn't easy to do.

The following week passed as usual, including my work, children, grandchildren, and conversations, either about Jerry or with him.

As Jerry and I discussed the new people in our lives, we would talk negatively about them one day and defend them the next. All along, I never let him know that I was no longer seeing or talking to Mr. Intelligence.

The game the two of us were playing became like a cat and mouse fight. I wanted to believe in Jerry at times, but there were others around me that just wouldn't let me forget his unfaithfulness to me.

Jerry was still doing questionable things, and my rebellion and anger towards him were escalating to the point where I craved revenge against him.

It is embarrassing how the rebellion in both of us caused us to indulge in so much foolishness and drama. To make sure my Father God and my Lord Jesus Christ get all the glory, I must keep it real.

In prior times with Mr. Intelligence at the casino, he introduced me to a band whose lead singer was out of the Chicago area. I really enjoyed the talent of this band. My roommate and I had become close to these guys and made a habit of showing up whenever they played at the casino.

They were playing that week, and as usual, the two of us showed up on that Friday night.

I didn't have anything to be concerned about, even knowing that Mr. Intelligence would be there at his usual spot because I had believed everything, he told me about never giving a woman a second chance. So, to be honest, I wasn't looking for a relationship with him. I thought, and I wanted everything between him and me to be over. *So why not just go, enjoy a good meal, hear these guys I had enjoyed so much and return home for the weekend,* I told myself.

When we got there that night, one of the first people we saw around the bar listening to the band and being his usual self was Mr. Intelligence. I didn't say anything to him, but my friend walked over, and the two of them exchanged a few words. I remained in my spot on the other side of the bar and spoke to the band members on the stage, making eye contact with them as they played.

When the band took a break, they came down and greeted me the same as they did when Mr. Intelligence and I were together. They did their usual thing during their break and returned to the stage. Each musician could work magic with his particular instrument.

By now, I had become one of their greatest fans. I really appreciated their talent, both individually and as a group. After they finish their set that night, we all talked for a while, and then I was ready to go home.

Once my friend and I got into the car, she talked about her conversation with Mr. Intelligence. It had been a while since I had been to the casino or seen him. I did miss his humor and his inept ability to keep me laughing about one thing or the other. I braced myself to hear from her what negative comment he had to say about me. There wasn't one bad comment he had spoken about me, to my surprise.

All he said to her about me was how he missed me and felt he was in love with me. That was hard for me to believe because all I could remember was the emphasis he put on the fact that once a woman abandoned him, he was done with her. In my mind, that's where I should have been, in the; **I'm done with you** category.

Overwhelmed about what I was hearing, I just went home and fell into a deep sleep. I was tired, and my right breast was hurting pretty bad. During that next week, Jerry and I went through our same routine with no actual accomplishments or earnest conversation.

I was still trying to reach the man in Jerry I saw the year before we were married; but he was still determined that he would never be that man again. So believing that there was nothing for me to lose with Jerry that I hadn't already lost, I gave Mr. Intelligence a call.

To my surprise, he talked to me. It looked as if I wasn't in the I'm done category, after all. Just what this meant, I didn't know. But at this point, it was evident and clear, that I was getting nowhere with Jerry.

From the way things looked in my life with Jerry, there was no difference in our lives or real hope for reconciliation.

I wasn't and didn't seek the Holy Spirit for guidance at all. And I had neglected the many ways; HE had tried to give me to escape. So foolishly, in my anger and blindness by my bitterness, I *went for it,* with Mr. Intelligence.

I was headed for a world that gave God no glory or showed no faithfulness to my Lord and Savior for the next five months of my life. I got completely involved with this man and his small world of   . In ways, he treated me more like a man should treat a woman and far better than my husband, Jerry, was doing I thought.

In numerous ways, he treated me more like a man should treat *the woman in his life* than my husband Jerry had ever done. But the things I was now doing had quenched my walk with God, and I was in total darkness--on Satan's turf.

Mr. Intelligence could see the gifts of God in me so clearly that he was making plans for using those gifts in our future for self-elevation and promotion. He saw himself as the one who could manage those divine gifts to make a profit for him and me. But there was one problem... I didn't see a future. A future for me didn't exist at the time. I was at a standstill, living a **whatsoever life,** because my mind and heart somehow still focused on Jerry.

It wasn't as if Mr. Intelligence didn't know that my heart wasn't entirely into what I was doing. It was more like, because of the intimate things I was doing with him, I had gotten over Jerry. But the truth was, I was doing the things I was now doing because I wanted to hurt Jerry. I couldn't see this truth then...I was in darkness—*total spiritual darkness.*

Shamefully, I misused this man's affection for me, and I pushed Jerry further away, causing him to accept all the trips and gifts this new woman was lavishing upon him.

The months passed, and Jerry's insurance was renewed. Once again, I was covered.

Doctors discovered that the pain occurring so regularly in my right breast was due to two types of cancer. Mr. Intelligence was using all his intelligence to gather information about what was going on with me. Jerry was being his usual self, going about with his life and work, and offering very little support or comfort to me.

I learned my daughter-in-law was also dealing with an aggressive form of breast cancer and was in a fight for the life of both herself and her unborn child. It was a very confusing time in my life. I became numb and couldn't entirely deal with the fact that I had breast cancer.

My life at that time was a mess. I was overwhelmed with trouble. But it was easier for me to focus on what I needed to do for my daughter-in-law and my son's family.

So I was trying to stick with the plan I had made before my cancer was discovered and still relocate to Chicago, where they were, to support them in their crisis.

Mr. Intelligence and Jerry were telling me that they would both help me to relocate. I was in a mess.

I didn't know if I could believe, when it came to Jerry, what he was saying he would do. I believed Mr. Intelligence would help me, but there were times when his friends and their needs seemed to come before me.

All of my friends and family were still upset with Jerry and criticized him for neglecting me, especially Mr. Intelligence. When it came to my marriage with Jerry, he could tell me about it as if he had been there watching things as they happened all those years. It appeared that he had experienced everything in life; except a real relationship with God.

He could accurately point out negative things about Jerry that I was not ready to admit were true. He was so good at describing my life with

Jerry that he made it seems like a movie was being played right before his eyes with audio included.

It was apparent he had paid attention to everything I told him about Jerry and our lives together. That kind of attention I wasn't used to. In my pain from my disappointments and anger with Jerry, I had been an open book, emptying myself to this man, and like a container, he had taken it all in.

The comments Jerry was coming back telling me that this new woman was making about me made it clear that he was emptying himself out to her also. Each of us needed someone to take sides with us against the other, and it appeared that we both had found just that. Satan had made sure that we would be divided and had sent two people to come between us. When God gave Eve to Adam, His will was: **what God joins together, let no man put asunder**. Unfortunately, Jerry and my sin had allowed the devil to separate what I believed God had joined together. During one of Mr. Intelligence and my conversations about my life's story, he requested that when the movie about my life comes out, he wanted to portray himself in it. After that statement, he broke out with this big haughty laugh. I resented him for being amine him for his finding my life pains "funny."

The pain I had endured throughout my life and was still enduring wasn't funny at all to me. But Mr. Intelligence appeared to really enjoy laughing at my heartbreaking story.

It seemed that the hurts and pains of my life, was something someone could always get in a laugh about, I thought to myself.

Have you ever said or confessed something about a person who had hurt you, to someone, when you were in deep pain, and they would come back and repeat it to you?

But when they repeat it to you, it's made you want to defend that same person you just talked about. Mainly, because when they repeat what you said about that person, they make what the person did to you sound lower and dastardlier than it was. Thereby, causing you to feel like an idiot for letting the person do you the way they had done. You then find yourself wishing you had never told them anything at all...For at that moment, you feel as low as you did when the person first did what they did to you.

There were many times doing my conversations with Mr. Intelligence, that he made me feel like an unlearned school girl.

Had my battle to hold on to my marriage with Jerry caused me to revert to a silly young girl? I asked myself. Am I not a mature and experienced woman?

Mr. Intelligence made me feel ignorant whenever he would make any comments about how Jerry had treated me. Even thought, every comment he made about the way Jerry treated me was true.

Truth can be hard enough, just realizing it. Facing truth is much harder to do when you see it through someone else eyes.

But what could I say? Everything he said was true. All Jerry's actions clearly showed that he didn't love me as a man should love his wife. It wasn't like I didn't know that I deserved a lot better treatment than my husband was giving me. The fact was: *I was so in love and entangled with my husband that I couldn't see just how low I had allowed myself to go for him.*

The odd thing was, I had done what the bible teaches me to do, I thought. **Ephesians 5:22** commands, "*Wives, submit yourselves into your husbands, as unto the Lord.*"

As I look at it now, I hadn't included the verse which came before that one. Therefore, I had only a part of the truth. **Ephesians 5:21** says, "*Submitting yourselves one to another in the fear of God.*"

I was right about submitting myself to my husband. The problem was I didn't have a husband that was submitting himself to me in the fear and reverence of God.

It wasn't much I could say back to Mr. Intelligence because he was biblically correct about how Jerry was *in error* in the way he treated me. It wasn't like Mr. Intelligence was using the bible to school me or anything; it was just that he was so knowledgeable about life. And it was clear to him that Jerry didn't love me.

"This man doesn't love you," he would say. He could always effectively make his point because Jerry always did something to prove his lack of love for me.

My battle with the invader called cancer was going to prove to me in another way; that Jerry didn't care for me as a husband should. **Ephesians 5:25** tells husbands this: *"Husbands, love your wives, even as Christ also loved the church, and gave himself for it;"*

Once I received insurance coverage again, and the doctors found two different cancers in my right breast. I was informed that I wasn't going to relocate to Chicago and help my son and his family. The doctors relayed to me how my hands would be full just trying to take care of myself during the battle I had to face with this invader called *cancer.*

This was something that I didn't know how to deal with at the time. To make matters worse, I received a phone call informing me my daughter-in-law was going into early labor with the baby. In so many ways, I knew that wasn't a good thing. I took this news with one thing on my mind...I've got to get there.

The doctor encouraged her to abort the baby to decrease the risks for the mother. There were so many problems with the baby not properly developing. Because of this, the doctor thought it would be best just to abort the baby. Of course, my daughter-in-law refused to abort her baby despite all the risks she would encounter by carrying it to full term.

Around that time, I found out that Jerry's insurance had a clause that stated we had to pay the deduction before the insurance would pay their 80% for the treatment, I needed to deal with the breast cancer. The deductible added up to $5,000.00. It was clear that no one in my life at that time could come up with that kind of money.

It was pathetic how I had not cried out to God because I was so frustrated and angry about how my husband had treated me. It had been over ten months now since our separation. The only thing both of us had done was grow further and further away from God's plan for our lives.

Yet, I was reminded in my *spirit man* that Jesus was still at the right hand on the throne of God, interceding for me.

Hebrews 7:25 reads, *"Wherefore he (Jesus) is able also to save them (me) to the uttermost that come (I had come) unto God by him, seeing he (Jesus) ever liveth to make intercession for them (me)."*

God was still showing me favor. **Proverbs 16:15** reads, *"In the light of the king's countenance is life, and his favor is as a cloud of the latter rain."* God had assigned the head surgeon and nurse that would be removing my breast. They were of his choosing.

This nurse was contacting everyone she knew (and she learned many people in high places), trying to find a way to get past the $5,000 deduction. It had been almost two months since the cancer was found, and nothing she had tried or done, or no one she had contacted, was offering any answers for the help I needed.

It was looking hopeless. The nurse then found a program that would be able to help me. It came down to just one problem... How do I qualify for this program? I had to not have any insurance to get the help, but I had insurance. That was the mountain now that I now needed to climb.

What a mess! Here I had waited seven months to get back on Jerry's insurance to get the medical assistance to find the breast's problem, and now I needed to go back to not having insurance to get the treatment I needed for the surgery. This type of problem was just one of the many kinds of issues I've faced all of my life. It always seems as though, what doesn't usually happen to others, ever happens to me.

With this all going on, I was actively in an adulterous affair with a man that had no interest in ever living what we saints call a *godly life.* At the same time, the man whom I was married to, who had the role of being my covering, was busy in the bed with another woman. Actually, by now, Jerry played more of the part of being the other woman's husband.

In the middle of this drama, I had a daughter-in-law fighting for the life of her and her baby. While I needed to be focusing on how to fight for my life against this invader called cancer, a myriad of dilemmas were bombarding my mind.

Then a ray of light appeared to finally come through concerning how I could get my breast surgery. A voice mail by the nurse who God had used to work so diligently on my case was left on my phone. She sounded excited and wanted me to call her as soon as possible. When I did, she informed me that there was a way that I could likely get from under Jerry's insurance. The course was this: Jerry would have to leave his job and be unemployed for at least 30 days so the insurance would lapse.

This seemed to be the perfect answer to her and all those she had consorted to get me the help I needed. But there was just one problem these people hadn't figured on facing... the problem was Jerry. This request was one that Jerry had no plans of being a part of. It seemed to him that this was just too much to ask him to do. Long story short: Jerry refused to give up his job, even when it could mean saving my life.

Even the people at Jerry's job were trying to figure out just what action to take to get the help I needed to have the surgery.

God was so merciful to me that Jerry's manager promised him that if he quit so that I could have the necessary surgery, they would hire him back after 30 days of him being unemployed by them.

So, his income would continue doing those thirty days, and his manager would pay him his vacation time and sick leave pay. For even more assured for my husband, God had one of his former co-workers, who had left the job where he now worked, contact him. This co-worker's current employer was looking to hire someone under him in his new leadership role at the company where he worked. He was sure that Jerry was the man for the job.

This would have been the ideal answer for someone trying to get his wife's help and wanted to make more money doing so. If Jerry had taken the job under his former co-worker, he would still have been employed when he left his current job for thirty days. With that proposal, Jerry would be hired as a new employee; this meant that he would receive coverage for himself without waiting 30 days to get reemployed.

Knowing Jerry's work ethic, this former co-worker wanted Jerry on his team. To my surprise, he did go and fill out the application there, but he still had no plan of leaving his current job, no matter what help I needed. He was currently working in a leadership position as a head maintenance tech at his current employment. No one knew, as well as I did, just how hard Jerry had worked to obtain that supervisor position.

He had about three or four people working under him at the time. Being in this leadership position made him just a step away from working in a higher supervisor role made available because of this same guy leaving, who was now trying to hire Jerry on his team.

I knew that Jerry had worked hard to get the opportunity to fill that supervisor role which was now open. Going under this former co-worker wasn't a part of Jerry's plans, even though he wasn't happy about some of the things he had to deal with as a lead technician with his current employer.

My battle with cancer depended on what Jerry would now do. Mr. Intelligence also knew about a maintenance position that Jerry could probably get within the management company he was currently employed with. He was aware of the problem of me needing the $5,000 for surgery. During our conversations about my husband, I had shared with him how good Jerry was in his field.

I once stated that, even if Jerry's had the inability to be a good husband, he still had the capacity of having a good work ethic. And when it came to his job, he always gave 100%, no matter where he worked. (As a matter of fact, Jerry's giving 100% to his employers and not his wife was one of the reasons that had caused our separation).

"If he's as good as you say he is, Joann, I'm almost sure I can get him in to talk with the right people to get this job," Mr. Intelligence told me. "If it means you getting the help you need, I'm willing to do whatever I can to help you."

It looked as if God had opened doors in more than one way to assure my husband that he didn't have to worry about having a job. But Jerry just wasn't willing to leave his job. It seemed he didn't care that refusing to take any of the offer's opinions being presented to him even if it could mean death for me.

I knew my husband well. I never saw those ideas and lucrative offers as an answer for me. Our marriage was the way it was because Jerry was incapable of putting my needs before his own. What he wanted would always come first. He had proven this to me throughout the three and half years we were married. Jerry was never going to place me or my health above his employment. This would have meant him making a sacrifice that would have been for my good. Doing what was suitable for me, my husband had already proved to be incapable of.

I knew he wasn't going to do it. Even in my sickness, he refused to make the sacrifice to get me the help I needed. His job was more important than me getting help to battle this invader attacking my body...after all, he wasn't the one who was sick.

"I'm sorry, Joann," is what Jerry said to me, "but I just can't see myself letting my job go, even if it's only for 30 days." Some people in my life knew about Jerry's decision not to help me. I wouldn't let most of the people in my life know because I was ashamed of the truth; he valued his job more than my life. I was now sickening and ashamed of what my whole life seemed to have become because of my love for this man.

Since most of my family members didn't know about the options, Jerry had to bail me out. Some worked hard to come up with different ideas to raise or acquire the money for my surgery.

Family members from other states were trying to get me to where they lived to get help. Even my wonderful daughter-in-law wanted me to come to Illinois. It seemed now that she was more concerned about me than she was about her own condition. I was devastated because I could not be there to support and help her in her crisis.

Since Blue Cross and Blue Shield covered me, a national insurance company, I felt that it didn't matter what state I relocated to. They would require the same thing. I was still going to show up as covered under Blue Cross and Blue Shield and would have to come up with the $5,000 deductible before getting the surgery needed to remove the cancerous breast.

If Mr. Intelligence and my close friends had any doubts before that Jerry didn't love me, it was no question now of the fact. Everyone who knew what was going on told me how my husband

couldn't love me and do what he was doing. Many now believed he hated me.

Jerry chooses to remain employed, even though his manager had assured him that she would hire him back, and Jerry not taking the job that a former co-worker was almost running him down to get him to take; was making him look terrible and proving to all that he didn't love me.

Even Mr. Intelligence was pretty sure that Jerry could probably get an interview and a job at the place where he worked. Jerry, having three opportunities to secure the surgery I needed and maybe even save my life, but he refused all offers.

I was overwhelmed with voices telling me how my husband couldn't love me, and I knew the voices were echoing the truth. I knew that all of them were right. Yet, what could I do about it? It was Jerry's insurance and Jerry's job. He only had the power to decide to let the job go to stop the coverage qualifying me for the women's **breast program.**

Without Jerry's willingness to let his job go, it looked as if the only option left for me was to somehow come up with the money.

Seeing no way to come up with the $5,000, I was going through a tough time both physically and mentally. My daughter-in-law, over 500 miles away, was also having a hard time with her condition. I was spending a lot of time, privately, in tears.

What my daughter-in-law was going through was breaking my heart. It was only when my breast was hurting badly that I would allow my problems to enter my mind.

I was still talking with Jerry almost every day, and he was still nonchalant and unconcerned about my condition. He was not exerting any effort to help me find a solution to my problem.

Why do you even talk to him? I was being asked by those who loved me and were concerned about my dilemma.

Family members were vexing me by asking me why I wouldn't leave the state and come to where they were. And the fact that I had been without work for a few months and had no income was hitting me hard, also.

Even though I was going through these dilemmas, the childish phone calls were still coming from whoever this small-minded person had been harassing me. Most of the time, I would not answer the phone when I saw no reference to calling. But there were times when I would answer the phone without noticing that it was that devil from hell on the other end.

The caller always called in a way where her number could not be tracked—that coward.

"What am I to do Lord," I cried out!

There were those moments where I was so overwhelmed, I found myself still calling on the name of the LORD, even in my mess. I had now stopped going to my father in the ministry church, back in my hometown, because I did not have the gas to put in the car. So, I would visit the church where I had served as the associate pastor. Everyone within that ministry was supporting me in my illness and praying for my daughter-in-law to be healed. Sometimes they would even help me out financially. But something was going on in me that wasn't being fulfilled. I was beginning to feel so much more condemned than I had been when I was having my affair and living in sin.

I had also started to visit another ministry in the Memphis area. This ministry was larger than what I used to, but it wasn't new to me because I knew the pastor and had been blessed by hearing him at a church occasion. I had been with the ministry I attended doing my years in Wisconsin.

I also met Bishop T. D. Jakes there, at this ministry, before Bishop Jakes relocated his ministry to Dallas.

This was during those years before Bishop Jakes became the preacher he is today. He wasn't a bishop at that time either. I purchase one of his first recordings for $20 of his "Women Thou Art Loose" series. That seems now so long ago in my life. When I purchased that series from Bishop Jakes, I remember saying to him how God had shown me while he was speaking during the service earlier that He would do something great in his life.

Bishop Jakes responded by asking me to pray for him. *You have no idea the type of attacks that I'm under. Please, he asked, share this with as many other women as you can. At church, in bible groups, any way you can, he asked.*

The strange thing was, I did understand in some ways what he meant about being under attack because of what other saints I knew and I were going through.

Many ministers, even I, were enduring adversity and hardships from within and without the church.

At that very same "Gospel Explosion" event, the church pastor I was visiting, T.D. Jakes and one other minister were being heavily attacked.

Bishop Jakes sold tapes that night, after service, after dealing with some of those attacks. People had even attacked his wife, gossiping about the way she was **dressed. But thank God, Bishop Jakes confronted some of** those issues when he spoke in that night's service. Then he addressed the sermon that God had given him that he had on the tapes. After hearing what he said was on the recordings, I knew that whatever was on those tapes was for me back then.

The oppression I was getting from the church I was attending during that conference was my clue that I needed more understanding on why I was going through some of the things I was confronting in life. There were many things that I was going through that I needed to go through; for me to be shaped and molded into the woman Christ wanted me to be.

Legalism in the church had put a yoke around my neck, of which I needed to be free. From the little information he gave during that night's service, I knew I needed the messages he had prophetically recorded on those tapes. By listening to those tapes, I would be given a better understanding of what was going on in my life as a woman of God.

I must have those tapes, I said to myself. From the small crowd that stood in line with me to purchase those tapes that night, it looked to me as though many people in that conference weren't responding to what the man of God had said about the messages in this tape album. I knew that God had something to say to me as a woman, and from what he eluded about those tapes, I knew I wanted and had to have them to share with all the women I knew.

With his wife by his side, he gave more insight into the information on the series of tapes I had purchased the night before during the breakfast conference the next morning. I noticed that only myself and one other brother from our Wisconsin group attended the conference that morning.

During that time, I felt that God was moving our Lord Jesus Christ's ministry into a more in-depth and different level than most saints could even fathom or comprehend. It appeared that there were many issues that the church had never been brought out so straightforward and direct before, as new revelations were being revealed. The pastor of the church I was visiting was serving under his father at the other church they had.

A lot of disunity and confusion within my church community at that time started happening. *Who was right and who was wrong? Who was in God's will and who was not?* Some of the elders, pastors, leaders, many of the older members and younger people are standing up and taking sides on specific issues that I believed God was addressing in the church.

I felt issues brought to light in messages such as those on those tapes hadn't been brought to the church's surface before. Even though this appeared to many to be great work from God, it appeared to be heresy to some in our mix.

Some people were attacking the men and women of God who were bringing these new revelations into the church, accusing them of being out of the will of God. But not me. I knew Jesus was getting answers to many who were praying for *truth, wisdom, and understanding* within the Body of Christ.

It was as if Jesus was leading godly men and women to uncover and address some of those legalistic issues in the church, in an unorthodox way at that time.

People were being used to bring unaddressed issues to light and expose hidden corruption and issues hidden under the rugs. This *shake-up* in the church, in many ways, is still going on today.

God was stirring and cleansing His church. Bringing a word through some men and women of our generation would finally help His people, not just to be saved but also to be delivered from legalism and bondage. Hungry souls were not only receiving a **"word"** from the **LORD**, but they were also getting to understand.

Many answers that I had asked, and others had long to receive from God, were finally being answered. God had heard and answered the cries of his people who were longing for deeper understanding--of precisely who they were, in Christ Jesus.

This ***new movement,*** some called it, that Bishop Jakes and others were ushering in was not the work of God; many in our church leadership were crying out. But that just wasn't true. God was in this new movement; I was sure of it

There will always be someone the devil will use to go too far in their revelation of God's word, and *error will occur*. But the truth of God's word will always prevail.

I believe that the messages like **"Woman Thy Art Loosed"** that I purchased from Bishop Jake that weekend were just the beginning of me taking Jesus and the Word of God out of the box. God was helping other women and me through those tapes; to understand some of the reasons we react the way we do, even though we had given our lives to Christ and had been born again in the spirit. God was moving on our generation. I believed His people were suffering from unfolding issues and problems. Which hadn't been addressed in the church or voiced from the pulpit before.

Many of God's people were suffering and were not getting the answers to their problems, as they suffered silently in the church. And I was one of them. Many things about the true issues of the heart, mind, body, and soul of the saints were off-limit and were not being addressed by the church's spiritual leaders.

I was sure and more than confident that God was building up men and women in churches throughout the nation to proclaim the truth and address issues that had been taboo and forbidden to be discussed behind the pulpit.

This new breed of prophets rising in our midst was being persecuted and attacked by the leaders who wanted to maintain the status quo. These leaders tried to stop these rebels or protestors, but God would not allow this because this movement was of God.

Understanding, wisdom and new insight were coming from Jesus through the word of God, addressing and dealing with the silent cries of this new generation of true believers that wanted to serve God with all their heart and in spirit and truth.

It had to be more to what Jesus had purchased for us by Him dying on the cross for us other than salvation, and we truly wanted to know what all that **more** meant for our lives.

Issues like how we dressed and what we wore seemed to take precedence over weightier matters. The focus should have been on the Word of God, cleaning up the inside of our bodies, and changing our lives. We needed instruction on sanctification and making us better people in our church, homes, and communities.

The goals of maintaining a sanctified appearance ranked above and even took priority over men and women being holy and righteous on the inside and over the inner man's sanctification. Those rules of keeping up the outside appearance were being forced down our throats and had become a significant burden to myself and others, who loved God and truly believed in our Lord and Savior Jesus Christ.

It seemed to me that so much emphasis was on what we *could not do* that barely any instructions were given about how we should be living. We needed practical instructions on how we could accomplish what Christ has commanded us to do in his Word. I felt like so many rules were held over our heads that it was as though a dark cloud was holding me in spiritual darkness and bondage. I felt the teachings that I was receiving from the church had very little to do with the liberty that the bible was teaching that I had in Christ. *My conclusion was that; it was way too much focus on the law.*

And from the messages being dealt with in the conference that weekend, it appeared that I wasn't the only one who thought this. Jesus's death has paved the way for a new and abundant life for every repentant soul who would come to him to be covered and saved by His blood.

Even at that time, I knew that how one dressed or looked was not a problem with God and wasn't a crucial issue to dwell on.

However, God and women of God should dress modestly and wear appropriate attire to tempt or entice the opposite sex.

I knew other fellow Believers thought as I did. All we wanted was to get some real-life answers to our challenges of living this new life in Christ.

By studying God's word, I observed that there were more instructions to living and overcoming many of the issues of life that the pulpit had not addressed. I wanted to know and understand how to have more victory in this world through our Savior and Lord Christ Jesus.

My fellow Christians and I just wanted to know what we needed to do to achieve and live that abundant life of victory in Christ.

Instead of us getting answers that brought a more profound and better understanding about our new life in Christ, it appeared that many of life's serious issues the saints wanted to have addressed were not addressed. Finally, it was as if God said, *"No More"* through the ministry of men and women like Bishop T. D. Jakes and others.

The deeper issues of life which I was seeking back then for, when I purchased that tape series from Bishop Jakes; in some ways, *I am still **seeking for** now.* Numerous times, I just wanted to pack up and leave the church I was in.

The spirit of legalism, boldly espoused by the church leaders, spoke of church hoppers' disastrous fate (those who visited different churches); and this froze me in fear and would not allow me to leave the church I was in.

Looking back over my life--not going to other churches and being a part of the people in God who was opening life issues like Bishop T.D. Jakes and this pastor, who I was visiting at that time, were among the biggest misstates I made.

I often wonder if I had relocated to a more ***word-centered*** church back then (I have lived to regret not moving to Dallas back then with T. D. Jakes) would I have been in the mess I was now in... ***Only God knows.***

Yet the fact was clear; I was now in a mess that appeared to be beyond any situation I had experienced or encountered before. I have been in some tight, dire, dreadful situations in my life, even more than I care to even remember or talk about at this time. Yet all of them seemed small to the mess I was now in, and to this invader, I would have to fight to preserve my very life.

I CAME TO MYSELF

Luke 15:17-18 says, "And when he came to himself, he said. I will arise and go to my father, and will say unto him, Father; I have sinned against heaven, and before thee." Like the prodigal son, in the story told by our Lord and Savior Jesus Christ, I would come to myself; I just didn't realize it now. **All my mess** had overtaken me, and I felt I was now in a murky pit eating with the hogs. It had happened to me so silently and gradually that I couldn't realize it, and I didn't quite know how it had happened. **But thanks be to God!!!** By His Mercy and Grace and **the invader called cancer,** my eyes were about to open.

The Word that was coming out in this ministry that I was now visiting in the Memphis, Tennessee area was about to awaken something down in my soul. I perceived this pastor as someone who had a deep spiritual understanding when I first met him when I met T.D. Jakes. But now, many years had passed. The revelations from his pulpit showed me that he had indeed grown even stronger in God's Word.

The first Sunday I visited his church, he recognized me in the congregation. I greeted him after service that day, and he gave me the last two Sunday messages alone with the one he had recorded that service. He asked that I listen to them. It appeared that he was still relating to the woman he had met and briefly talked to years before, assuming that I had the maturity in God to judge whether I should come back to his church or not--by what I heard on those recordings.

He said, "Listen to them, Sister Joann, and then decide if this is where you need to be?" He had no way of knowing just how far I had gotten away from being that spiritual woman of God I was long ago, but God knew.

The moment I got into the car, I began to listen to the first tape of the word the pastor had preached two Sundays before my visit.

I kept playing each sermon repeatedly: In my car, in the house; over and over, God's word was coming through those messages I was hearing and going straight to my spirit and soul. Little did I know or realize that my body was also being nourished--and *slowly but surely*, was being healed by the **Word of Truth**.

Ezekiel 36:26-27 prophesies, *"A new heart also will I give you, and a new spirit will I put within you: and I will take away the stony heart out of your flesh, and I will give you a heart of flesh. And I will put my spirit within you, and cause you to walk in my statutes, and ye shall keep my judgments, and do them."*

I began to share with Jerry about what was happening to me by hearing this man of God's words. I felt no reason to relate to Mr. Intelligence about what was happening to my spirit and soul because I felt, he would not understand.

I didn't think he would even care or try to understand what I was experiencing.

But I was eager to share this information with Jerry, who seemed excited about what God was doing in my life. As I'm looking back now, I realize that my eagerness to share what was happening to me with Jerry--had to do with the hope that this information would also start to revile his *spirit.*

With all I had gone through with Jerry, it still didn't stop me from talking with him or loving him. Sometimes I would call Jerry, but other times he would call me.

The decision that he made *not to let the job go* so I could get the help I needed would sometimes come up. Then we would start all over again with **who did who wrong**, and the fight was on. Yet this didn't stop us from talking to each other regularly.

That following Sunday, I was right there sitting among this pastor's congregation. The series that

I listened to was continued the next day. The Holy Spirit was calling out to me, but I couldn't go up and join this man's church; knowing the life of sin, I was still living with Mr. Intelligence. But I couldn't stop attending the services I would go to every Sunday and Wednesday night.

Jerry checked with me daily to inquire about my health and ask me about the word that this pastor had preached during the Sunday and Wednesday night's service. He was acting as if the story that I was hearing and sharing was affecting him also. Even though we were both in open relationships with someone else, there seemed to be some unexplainable connection with the two of us when it came to the Word of God.

Several months passed by, and I couldn't stay away from this pastor's services. But I couldn't join his ministry either. Not with what I was doing.

I would attend this pastor's service early every Sunday morning, and when the service was over, I would go to the ministry where I had been an associate pastor and attend the rest of their morning service.

It was as if I needed all the words I could get from both churches. I was gradually eating more and more of God's word. I started to get back into my bible. This pastor gave out assignments during our Sunday morning services and the Wednesday night bible class. So, I had to start studying God's word again.

I found myself still visiting Mr. Intelligence even as I was getting back into reading my bible. The assignments that we were getting on Wednesday nights caused me to research and study God's word now, even when I was spending the night sleeping with Mr. Intelligence. It didn't seem to affect Mr. Intelligence at all, but it was affecting me.

It had been almost two months now since learning that the surgery to amputate my right breast couldn't be done until I came up with the $5,000. No matter how often or how much Jerry and I talked, he still wasn't changing his mind about letting his job go to help me.

When peopled asked me what was going on with my situation, I would just say, "God got it." And that was all I could say.

My visits to the casino with Mr. Intelligence had now become a rare event. Most of the time, I stayed at his place while he went alone or with some of his friends. Since I didn't have my place, Mr. Intelligence's apartment had become like my own. He would allow me to change things around to look the way I like things to look.

It was easy for me to spend time in the Word of God whether I was at his place or my girlfriend's home because they both worked, and I had no job.

I was still trying to carry on my role as a mother and grandmother as much as I could. But with no income coming in at all, it was getting harder and harder for me to play my role as my *family's helper; and their way out* of whatever financial situation they had gotten themselves into.

I visited this new church so much most people related to me as one of the members. And to be honest, I would feel like one when I was among them. But the real-life I was living never let me forget the failure I was in God. I was sick with cancer that was spreading more and more in my body. I had no money and couldn't work to make any. I was foolishly taking a chance every day of dying and spending eternity in hell I felted.

I was hurting everywhere. My *body, mind, heart,* and *soul* were perpetually in pain. Yet, for the first time as a woman or even as a young sexually acted girl, I had finally found a man that was able to fulfill my every thought, idea, and desire and tame that unruly sexual beast within my body. Mr. Intelligence appeared to the answer for that sexual "thing" within me.

Not only did he recognize my addiction, but he understood it and knew how to handle it, as no man before him had done. I had never totally allowed God to have my body and take control of this sexual devil within me. Neither did I want to let that part of me go.

Rev. 3:20 reads, *"Behold, I stand at the door, and knock: If any man (this includes man and female) hears my voice, and open the door, I will come into him and will sup with him and he with me."*

I wasn't trying to get delivered from this part of me. I didn't realize anything was wrong with me in that area of my life. I just thought and accepted it as me just being who I was. **Thinking like this, I was only deceiving and fooling myself.**

If I had genuinely believed that this was just a part of who I was, I wouldn't have kept marrying all those different men to keep from sinning again God in this area of my life. My mind and mouth were saying one thing, but my actions in handling that part of my life spoke out about how I felt about that sexual devil within me.

Anything in your life or your flesh with more power over you than you have over it is ***not of God***.

Paul teaches in **Galatians 5:16-19a**, *"This I say then; walk in the spirit, and ye shall not fulfill the lust of the flesh. For the flesh lusted against the spirit, and the spirit against the flesh: and these are contrary to the other: so that ye cannot do the things that ye would. Now the works of the flesh are manifest, which are these; Adultery, fornication, uncleanness, lasciviousness...."*

Ephesians 5:3 says, *"But fornication, and all uncleanness or covetousness, let it not be once named among you, as becoming saints."*

Romans 6:13 reads, *"Let not sin therefore reign in your mortal body, that ye should obey it in the lusts thereof."*

Psalm 19:13 teaches, "Keep back thy servant also from presumptions sins; let them not have dominion over me: then will I be upright, and I shall be innocent from the great transgression."

Even though I had finally found a sexual mate that knew just how to handle that part of me, my spirit and soul had no peace or rest. The revelations and understanding that came from this new pastor I was listening to, along with the knowledge I already had of God, began to convict, agitate, and stir up something in the mix of my untamed sexual hunger--like nothing I had experienced before.

Foolishly for years, I had allowed myself to believe that the ability to control that thing in me would and could only come from a man with whom I was in love.

Now, the **truth** was right before me.

I was still in love with my husband, but this man was the one that made my sexual life appear to be whole. I could separate true love from true sexual satisfaction I didn't understand, and it confused me even more. But the one thing that was becoming stronger and stronger in my life was that I just couldn't go on living without totally giving up *everything* to God.

The fleeting moments of sexual pleasure with this man were being overcome by a longing to know God even more and understand Jesus' role in my life. I wanted now to allow the Holy Spirit to lead me and guide me into all truth truly.

I had been trying to find a way to make what I had with this man fit into my life with God. I now could see that this is what I had done with every man I had had before him.

With Mr. Intelligence, the promise I had made would never try to get another man to believe and live his life for God; I could easily keep.

Mr. Intelligence had experienced so-called saints in his life before. I presumed that nothing I could do or say to change his way of thinking when it came to God because of all the hypocrisy he had experienced before I came along.

For years I had been a victim, bound by sexual addiction. In many ways, this controlled my life and caused me to make wrong decisions with men repeatedly.

But now, I found myself in a place where even my sex addiction couldn't temporally satisfy or make me whole.

Unlike the past years of my life, when I could live in a false allusion that *at least I had something in my life the way I wanted it,* I was now standing and looking at myself with honest eyes and facing reality.

The following statement may sound crazy to all of you who are sound in the Lord. For those struggling with any addiction or who lack revelation or real understanding of who God is and what Christ has done for us, and what God requires of us—this statement will make sense.

I prayed to God this*: God, I now realize that I can't free myself from this sexual bondage (addiction) that I am in, but I need your help. The temporary pleasure of sin does not satisfy me, but it is only creating in me a deeper emptiness and longing for You. More and more each day, Lord Jesus, I realize I need you more and more and that only you can satisfy or deliver me.*

I was sitting alone, in Mr. Intelligence's crib, overwhelmed with all the thoughts which were going on inside of me when God started revealing Himself to me.

My phone rang, and I answered. It was the nurse that God had assigned to my case, trying to find a way to help me. She said that she had received a call from the Chief Financial Officer of the place that had seen the cancers in my right breast. This nurse couldn't forget me, partly because I had two different cancers in one breast. The nurse wanted to know how I was doing.

The nurse began to inform the CFO that I was having a problem with the deduction clause in my husband's insurance and that I didn't have the $5,000 needed to pay the deduction. She informed the CFO of the many different people she had talked to, trying to get around the deduction problem.

She told me how she explained to this woman that the only possible way around the problem appeared to be my husband leaving his current job for at least 30 days. I would then have no insurance, so I could in turn, qualify for the program. As I listened, the nurse told me that she had also relayed to this woman about the offer that my husband had received from his current employer and the other employment doors offered him, but he had refused them all.

The nurse shared with me the reaction of this lady. Once she was informed, my breast had not been removed (which she was sure had been done by now). This lady was angry because the evidence in my medical reports led this woman to conclude that removing that breast was of urgency and should have been done as soon as possible after the cancers were discovered. At present, the cancers have been diagnosed for over three months.

To find out that the cancers were still within my body after three months of being discovered was more than this woman could comprehend or stomach.

I knew what was going on. God was moving upon this woman's heart, and this was causing her to act right away.

She informed my surgical nurse to set up my surgery immediately.

She gave the nurse the instructions to follow once I came in to start the necessary paperwork for the surgery. I was given a date for my surgery. I was instructed on what I needed to do before the day of the surgery.

I was instructed to inform anyone asking about the $5000 to contact the CFO at the medical center where the cancer was found and give her name. I was careful to write down each instruction.

When I hung up the phone with this nurse, I was overwhelmed. I was overwhelmed this time because I knew that God was on my side for a surety.

Psalm 124:1-8 reads, *If it had not been the LORD who was on our* (my) *side, now let Israel* (Joann) *say If it had not been the LORD, who was on my* (her) *side when men* (Jerry wouldn't do what a husband should do for me) *rose up against us* (me): *then they* (cancer and all I got myself into from the loss of my marriages) *had swallowed us* (me) *up quick when their* (Jerry's) *wrath was kindled against us* (me) *when the waters* (all of my situations) *had overwhelmed us* (me), *the stream* (my troubles) *had gone over our* (my) *soul: then the proud* (raging) *waters* (all I had done and was doing in my life out of my anger against Jerry) *had gone over our* (my) *soul. Blessed be the LORD, who hath not given us* (me) *as a prey to their* (the devil's and the hell I had opened my life to by allowing my anger against my husband to take me entirely out of the will of God) *teeth. Our* (my) *soul is* escaped *(the word of God was bringing me to a place in God that I had not been before)* as a bird out of the snare of the fowlers: the snare is broken, and we *(Joann)* are escaped. *(I was beginning to come out of my ungodly mess).* Our *(my)* help is *(yesterday, today, and forever)* in the name of the LORD, who made heaven and earth.

The Lord's unmerited favor was working on my behalf through this **CFO** by using her authority and the position she had to get my cancerous breast removed. I sat overwhelmed in my chair after I hung up the phone. All I could do was weep. There were no words that I could think of that could tell my LORD how I felt. So, I just said,

"Thank You..."

I told Mr. Intelligence and my family about the date that had been set for my surgery. I didn't explain how it had become possible for me to have the surgery done when only $5000.00 could make the surgery happen. But those who knew God knew that it was only HIM who had made this surgery possible.

It was ironic how Jerry could praise God for my surgery and have no regret that he had nothing to do with me getting it.

Family members and friends began to change their schedules to be with me the day of my surgery; Mr. Intelligence was determined to be there too. Jerry wasn't sure that he could make it to the surgery but promised he would be praying for me whether he was there or not.

Jerry had no fear or emotions when I told him Mr. Intelligence was planning on being there by my side.

Jerry wasn't going to go to his job for any reason, and he wasn't going to miss a day from it either.

My son wasn't going to be able to leave Chicago. All the things his wife was going through with her battle with breast cancer made this impossible. She was putting up a great fight and forever encouraging me to do the same. I was still in a stage of not focusing on my situation because I was more concerned about her and the baby.

My daughter-in-law was doing all that the bible encourages a saint to do when fighting. Her mother had taken a leave of absence from her job to be there for her and my son and grandson. I was relieved that she was there, but I wanted to be there also. My daughter-in-law only wanted me to fight for myself and not to worry about her.

My fight wasn't as much about cancer; I was excited about how now I was getting back into the will of the LORD. I was getting back into the place with God that I had been before. But that wasn't what was happening. I was becoming a new creature:

Not just a woman who says she loves God, but one who was now falling in love with the LORD.

The surgery day was coming up fast, and I wasn't sure what to think about it. Doctors ordered my entire breast to be removed, but this wasn't a problem because the breast was hurting me.

Mr. Intelligence and I discussed how I would do the things to take care of myself once that breast was gone. Yet, it all seemed foggy and a blank at that moment, the things I was going through. Even at this point, I was still unsure of what I would do about my spiritual life.

Mr. Intelligence would often bring up marriage and how he knew that his life would have to change for him to adequately provide for the people in my life and me that I cared so much about, the things that we needed.

I wasn't thinking at all about another marriage. In my past, that would have been my goal. But now, all I was thinking about was how fast I could have my surgery, so I could get to Chicago to help my son and daughter-in-law.

Since Mr. Intelligence had medical experience and had a family member that was a doctor, he would often try to talk with me about my condition and my daughter-in-law's. I would listen to him about myself, but I refused to hear any information about and of the possibility that she wouldn't be healed. He could see my love for her, and I think he was concerned about how I will react to my illness if anything happens to her. I knew that he was only trying to prepare me for what could happen from a medical point of view in his way.

But I would reject everything that didn't fit in with what God's word promises us. And he could see this.

I had a good relationship with Mr. Intelligence, and even though he was trying to comfort me and say all the right things and was doing what a man who loves a woman should do, I just couldn't see being married to him.

He would often talk to his family member, who was a doctor, about my case. He was always on the internet getting information about breast cancer to help me find a cure. He had even Googled information on my doctor and was pleased with how my surgeon ranked in his field.

Mr. Intelligence was trying to prepare us both for life after the surgery. It's kind of strange how he could show me affection and then laugh at my emotional pain (which was brought on by the way Jerry was treating me) at the same time. Sometimes he would be so passionate and understanding, and at other times, he seemed to be cruel and thoughtless as he laughed and joked about how Jerry was abusing me.

At the beginning of this cancer nightmare, without even asking the LORD for what to do, He began to give me instructions on how He was about to assign a medical team to my care.

It had already begun with the surgeon and his head staff nurse, who had fought relentlessly to get me the operation for my breast. After the surgery, the help God had sent would consist of the cancer doctor, the nutritionist, the physical therapist, numerous pastors, ministers, prayer warriors, and family members and friends, who would be helping me fight that invader in my life.

The one thing that God made clear to me was that I would have to put all negative people out of my life. It didn't matter who they were. If anyone brought any negative actions or words to me, I was to pull myself away from them. It would be months down my *road of recovery* before I was able to do just that.

Mr. Intelligence, along with my surgical nurse, was trying to prepare me for what my life would be like after the surgery. As good as they explained things, nothing could ease the pain that my heart was suffering. I was trying to put up a good fight, but the emotional hurt brought on by the way my husband had treated me and was still doing me co tormented me and would not go away.

Mentally, I was trying to be fair to Mr. Intelligence and, with sincerity, demonstrate to him that I loved him because he was all I needed a man to be, in so many ways, **but I couldn't make my heart obey my mind.**

The Holy Spirit was now growing stronger and stronger within me, and I wasn't sure how long I would stay in that relationship with Mr. Intelligence. I tried not to hurt him, but I wanted to love and respect him because of the caring way he treated me, but I could feel he could see right through me. I had dug a ditch for myself that I had no idea how I would get out. I begin to cry out in my spirit, **"God help me, please!"** Little then did I know...**HE was doing just that.** By digesting God's word and from the tugging and wooing of HIS SPIRIT, *I was coming to myself.*

LOSING IN THE NATURAL, BUT GAINING SPIRITUALLY

On July 1 of 2009, I was at the hospital at 6 am. I was there to begin preparation for my surgery. So many different things were going on in my head. Even though I was alone now, others would come and be there before I came out of surgery.

To my surprise, Jerry showed up before he went to work. We didn't say much. We both looked each other in the eyes and thought about how messed up things had gotten between us. At least I did. I couldn't be sure what was on his mind. He took my hand, and I began to cry. Jerry then assured me that he would be checking back on me later.

"Call me," he said. I needed Jerry, and I wanted him to stay, but what could I say. I knew that Jerry wouldn't miss his job to stay at the hospital with me during the surgery. I wanted to tell him this, but there was no way I could say that out loud.

Inside, I knew if I did, it wouldn't make any difference anyway. Jerry had stopped giving me what I needed or wanted from him a long time ago.

This was not the day for more emotional and mental pain. So, I let it go. I was about to lose a part of my body, and only God knew what type of pain I would be physically feeling eight hours later.

As they took me back to get me ready for the surgery, one of the hospital workers asked me if anyone was with me. I softly answered, "They'll be coming later."

No one close to me was there to give me human comfort. I was there alone at the most frightening time of my life. There would be other surgeries in the future where I would be in this same situation-isolated and all alone.

The doctors and nurses introduced themselves to me and took me over the steps of what they would be doing and informed me of things I could expect.

Emotionally, I begin to fall apart. My surgeon came in and began to tell me again what he would do and approximately how long it would take. At the time, I didn't know what or how to feel. I just nodded my head in response to his questions; then, I laid there in silence until they started the **I.V.**

Just when I was ready to get things over with, the pastor of the ministry that was feeding me the Rhema (living word), which I needed to get my life back in order with my Loving God, came through the door. His wife was with him. They assured me that they had prayed for me and that they loved me. I needed them so badly, and it felt so good at that moment to know that someone, who loved God and loved me, was there in the room.

The first lady gave me a big hug. I really needed it. They then quietly left the room.

What I was now facing was hard. It was very, very hard. And I felt lost and all alone. Suddenly, the nurse came in, and I was off to surgery. Seven hours later, I awakened in recovery. I was by the doctor said that everything went well. I remember thinking: "For whom?"

The immensity of my physical problems finally hit me. I looked under my gown and saw white bandages and all these tubes coming out of pierced flesh; just as my surgeon had told me, I then lost it. I couldn't stop crying.

More people had now come to the hospital to see me: My best friends were there; my daughters were there; and one of my sisters was there, all waiting for me to come out of surgery. Family from everywhere had been calling and checking on me. Different pastors and many church members had been acquiring on my condition.

Someone told me that Mr. Intelligence had been there and stayed as long as he could before having to leave.

Nothing I heard could cheer me up or change how I felt about what had just happened to me. A part of my body had just been taken away. How would I look with only one breast? What was I going to do? Would I ever be the same again? No one could say anything that would change what had just happened to me. They all tried to say encouraging words, but it just didn't help.

The drugs they had given me for pain started to kick in, and I was *out-of-it* and oblivious until hours later. When I awakened, I remember seeing family and friends in the recovery room.

I nodded back off. And when I awaken again in my room, not sure how many hours had passed, I saw sitting in a chair on the other side of me: Mr. Intelligence.

Not knowing what to say, he made an inappropriate and *silly quote that he wouldn't know how he would feel if someone had taken a part of him away. Therefore, he continued telling me that I thought or acted would be okay,* but his tolerance for my emotional outbursts would only last a short time.

That week, Jerry was due to go to his family reunion out of town. And he did. Jerry called several times, checking on me during his trip.

He assured me that his family was sending their love, prayers, and support in his calls to me.

After calling him a few times, I detected his nonchalant attitude during the week, which made me feel like I was getting in the way of his trip, so I didn't call him anymore.

There were many things to learn about caring for the wounds and raw flesh where the pus and blood drained from me. Mr. Intelligence mainly did everything for me himself. He cleaned me up and encouraged me to do as much as I could on my own.

What I couldn't do, he did. He helped me to eat and would inform the staff on what I did and did not like. He was so helpful in my care that he became very popular with the people on my floor and throughout the hospital.

He was so attentive to me that everyone there thought that he was my husband. Who else but a husband would give a woman that type of care and support? But the problem was, he was not my husband.

Some of my family and friends concluded that since my husband was off doing his own thing, there was nothing wrong with me getting love, suppose care from this man?

In the eyes of God, I was another man's wife, but Mr. Intelligence wasn't reflecting on this at the time, but it never left my thought.

Finally, my hospital stay was over, and I was released to go home. Since I didn't have my place, and my girlfriend, whom I was living with, couldn't stay home and care for me, we decided I would stay with my sister at her home.

Another one of my sisters decided and came from Chicago to be with me and assist me doing my recovery period.

Mr. Intelligence would always make his rounds when he wasn't working. I became stronger to the degree where I could clean my wounds and empty my drains.

The time came for my sister and others to go, yet Mr. Intelligence stayed by my side.

When I went on my appointment to see my surgeon, the nurse came into the room, and she looked and saw my male friend sitting there. She immediately turned to me and asked, "Is this the man that I heard so much about from your hospital stay?" I responded, "It is." She looked at me and smiled.

Mr. Intelligence was wonderful in the care he gave me. However, he still had this thing about being negative towards people, and he usually had a pessimistic comment about everyone he met, even her.

The doctor had removed my breast. The next step was chemotherapy. Because my cancer was in the stage 3C category when they found it, there was no way around this procedure.

From August until December, every Monday of each week, there would be chemo treatments.

My daughter-in-law shared some of the side effects she was experiencing and how the chemo made her feel. But nothing my doctor and his staff or my daughter-in-law told me would quite prepare me for what I was about to face.

Every patient who goes through a particular surgery will not respond in the same way because

everyone's body, will, and personality are different. One person's body may be able to endure a particular drug or therapeutic procedure better than another person. No two people's bodies are exactly alike. After having the same treatment, one person may die, and another will live. Listen to your body: You will learn what you can and cannot take and how far you can and cannot go.

It's nothing wrong with having days where you just can't and don't feel like doing anything.

Just don't stay in that frame of mind.

No matter how good your caregivers are or how hard they try to take care of you, the battle is really left to you and God. God is your true help and Caregiver!

My daughters, my sister from Chicago, and one of my girlfriends, and her husband were there with me on my first visit with my cancer doctor after my initial surgery and stay-at-home recovery period. On my next visit to the doctor, my two sisters supported me, along with Mr. Intelligence.

During my first chemo treatment, only Mr. Intelligence and I were there. I got sick when they put that poison in my system, just as they had promised me.

The longer one stays sick, the fewer and fewer people who go with you to support you become.

It is not necessarily because people don't want to be there, but sometimes because they can't. People have to go on with their lives. No one's bills, problems, or any other obligations that come with life, stop because a friend or loved one gets sick. Not even the person who is ill.

I was still trying to live as normal of a life as I could.

When I couldn't drive myself to church, Mr. Intelligence was nice enough to guide me. This wasn't always a good thing because he recognized one of the sisters' praise team from his past.

He didn't care about where this woman was at now in her life or the fact that God's word had changed and redeemed her. He was focused only on her past. He began to tell me about the type of person she was when he knew her back in the

day. I really didn't care to know about her past. It wasn't like I could talk about her anyway since I was still living a life of hypocrisy with him; instead of defending the woman and telling him of the miraculous change God can make in one's life, I just let him talk.

Along with the medical team God had ordained and brought to me, there was also another team God put together and brought into my life. This team consisted of a group of prayer warriors.

Somehow, the pastor's mother, who had ordained me as an Evangelist a year ago, heard that I had cancer, and she solicited my phone number from a fellow ministry. I was elated and surprised both in my body and in my spirit when I got the call from her.

This lady had a three-way prayer line ministry where she would call and connect two other prayer warriors, and they would bombard heaven with a prayer for people. At the time, this was one of the greatest blessings that came into my life.

I wasn't brave enough to tell the mother about the sin and the dilemma I had gotten myself into concerning my marriage and illicit affair. Still, I was so grateful that she had obeyed God when He had solicited her to pray for me and to believe in my healing.

What was so remarkable about this prayer-line team was that prayer warriors and callers dialed in from all over the country. The only problem was when the connection was lost or someone got off of the phone, all calls would drop.

This prayer line ministry wasn't concerned about what denomination the person was in who needed help. It was just sisters and brothers that believed in the power of prayer and the word of God, who would intercede and bombard heaven for those with needs.

A sister in New York said that this mother was praying for who had cancer as I did. She and I became close to each other through praying over the phone and interceding for one another. The prayer partners were also praying for my daughter-in-law's recovery.

There would be times when the New York sister was in so much pain; I couldn't do anything but cry for her.

Not mother; there would be no emotional outburst for her. No matter how it looked or sounded, she would only pray what the Word of God said about healing. If the sister were in the emergency vehicle on her way to the hospital or there already, Mother would only believe and pray the Word of God.

The New York sister and I exchanged phone numbers, and many times we would call each other and talk and pray for each other. She knew about my daughter-in-law, and she prayed for her and believed in her healing.

Sometimes, I couldn't talk, so that she would speak and pray. And then there were *many more times* when she was extremely sick and in too much pain to say a word so that I would talk and pray.

About this time, I received calls about a fellow sister in the ministry where Jerry and I had served that also had breast cancer. She was having a hard time in her battle.

Through this new prayer line ministry, I became a part of other women diagnosed with cancer conditions.

During this time, I heard reports that my precious daughter-in-law wasn't doing well.

I was beginning to fall apart on what seemed like every side. But I couldn't let anyone know. I wasn't talking to Jerry much now because I didn't want to fight with him.

The harassing phone calls from the unknown and foolish woman, updating what Jerry and his new woman were doing, were still coming in.

I was now calling into the prayer-line more often, both as an intercessor and as a prayer warrior.

After God supernaturally opened the door for my surgery. He didn't stop showing out on my behalf even though I was still involved in my relationship with Mr. Intelligence. God changed my financial situation. Since April, I hadn't had an income since I quit my job with plans to move to Chicago and help my son and daughter-in-law.

In August, I received a letter from the social security office stating that I would be receiving disability starting in September. I had just applied for it in July. Whoever heard of a person getting social security benefit that fast? I read the letter over and over because I just couldn't believe how God was providing for me even when I hadn't submitted my _all_ to him.

A phone call came through a few weeks later about my daughter-in-law. I had just entered Mr. Intelligence's apartment, sat in a chair when my daughter called me. I asked my youngest daughter, who was on the phone, "What was that again, did you say?" "Call your son at his house.

Something is going on with his wife", she said. I immediately hung up and called.

I wasn't able to get my son on the line. I couldn't get my grandson, who stayed with them on the line either. I began to fall apart. Fighting back the tears, I sat there in the chair and kept trying to get through to my son. Finally, someone answered the phone at my son's house. She informed me that my daughter-in-law had just left in the ambulance to the hospital. My son was on his way to the hospital also. I asked where my grandchildren were? She told me that they were with the neighbors. She was also one of my son's neighbors, answering the phone at his home.

"What's going on?" I asked as I told her who I was. She answered and said to me that they had to take my daughter-in-law to the hospital. She went on to tell me that they didn't think she was going to make it. My heart stopped for a moment. The neighbor continued to say that her husband had taken my son to the hospital, and she should be hearing from them soon. She gave me her husband's cell phone number, and I immediately called.

The husband answered. I told him who I was and asked *if he could please tell me what was going on.* He told me that my daughter-in-law had just passed away. I sat back in my seat and began to talk to God.

Please, please, God, no! She believed in you and you alone. Lord, my daughter-in-law didn't allow any of us to think any other way. She always insisted that she was healed, trusting, and believing that you would heal her. What am I supposed to do now? **LORD**, what am I supposed to do?

I was confused.

Mr. Intelligence didn't say anything to me; he just let me cry. It wasn't long before my phone was ringing like crazy. *Is it true? Is it true?* My whole family was falling apart. It felt as if someone had taken my heart, and there was nothing left but this big hole. It was a very long night, and all I wanted was to be with her.

If I could just hold her one last time, hear her voice, and feel her arms around my neck. I wasn't prepared to let her go. I wasn't. If this saintly young lady believed in you the way she did, Lord, and you allowed her to die, what hope do I have?

I wasn't allowed the luxury to stay in this maze. My children and grandchildren needed me to be the bulwark that I had always been in a time of trouble.

The fact that I was in the middle of a battle with fighting cancer was suddenly placed aside. I stepped up to the plate and started reassuring everyone that called; *God will see us through this.*

I began to make plans necessary to get to my son. But inwardly, my mind was foggy and confused.

My prayer line warriors and mother called just when I needed her to. I explained to her what was going on. She began to tell me the words that she was receiving from God, "Base your condition on nothing but His word," *she said.*

I thought to myself, that's *just what my baby had done to God, and she's dead. Isn't that just what she did?*

Again, the mother began to speak, confirming what was in my spirit as if she had heard what I had just told God. "You are you, and your daughter-in-law was your daughter-in-law. We must always believe that God will heal us, but it is up to **HIM** to choose. Only believe what the

Word of God says, only speak and believe that", she admonished me.

God began to move and did just what I needed Him to do. My children, grandchildren, and I could go to Chicago to console the family and attend my daughter-in-law's homecoming services.

The next few months of my life were horrific and heartbreaking: The sister in New York passed away, and our prayer line mother for a moment wouldn't tell me this, knowing the devastating effect it would have on me. When she did tell me, I fell apart again.

With my social security checks consistently coming in, I finally got my place again. Mr. Intelligence and others in my life didn't think that this was what I should do.

I had to get my **closet and space** to be alone and get back to God. I was in no mood to try to explain this to anyone. I just needed to get into my place.

I cried every night about my daughter-in-law. The chemo was draining and wiping me out every time I received it. And I was now taking care of myself; since I was living alone, It was hard, very hard.

There was so much going on in my body, my heart, and inside my head.

I couldn't afford a car yet, so I had no transportation to get me back and forth from my many appointments.

Mr. Intelligence had a car, but it was being shared by several of his friends. He had his world, and now, since I was in my place, he just wasn't able to help me with all the new challenges that were coming my way.

When I got to this new place, I learned that I couldn't get utility services before paying an old bill that Jerry, my husband, had left with the utility company.

I was confused, *"What old bill?"* What bill did he owe?

I went down to the utility office to get the utility problem taken care of, and that is when it was revealed to me that Jerry had previously had an apartment which he didn't pay the bill on before he let it go.

This was the apartment he had when he got the dog, during the time I had been fighting with him about me keeping the house which I had acquired on my own—and had put so much of time and money into.

Jerry and I were married and supposedly living together. Still, he rented a house from his employer without me knowing about it. Jerry obtained an apartment but wouldn't let me have the house that I leased for myself. Jerry already secretly had this apartment he rented from his employer. He already had a place to go to, and now, this old bill was proof of it.

Upon finding this out, I went completely crazy. I realized Jerry allowed me to move from one place to another in my sickness when he had a place all the while.

I left that office in my fragile condition and headed right for his job. **I was ready to fight!**

All this hell going on in my life, and I find out this Negro had done this to me. This was just too much for me to take, so I headed to his job for a physical confrontation. I knew I wouldn't be able to win, but it just seemed to make sense to find him and just jump him until one of us couldn't fight anymore.

On my way to find him, Mr. Intelligence called to check on me. I began to tell him what I had just found out, and, as usual, he started laughing.

"This dude just didn't give a damn about you," he voiced between his chuckles.

Mr. Intelligence stopped laughing for a moment and began to try to calm me down. "I can hear it in your voice; you are ready to fight that Negro, aren't you," he said.

"Listen," he went on, "stop the car, pull over and think for a minute…What will this accomplish?"

"This man has hurt you enough. Don't let him keep on doing you this way. Just calm down, girl", he said.

Mr. Intelligence didn't realize that he was the next one on my list to beat-down because he laughed about something that was hurting me this bad. I pulled over and began to try to breathe. Now, I was angry with him also, and I no longer wanted to talk to him.

"What are you going to do," he asked?

"I don't know, but I don't have any money to pay an old bill for him," I voiced angrily.

The utility company's policy was; if you were married to someone at the time, they made a bill and the bill was left unpaid, you are then

responsible for that spouse's bill, whether the two of you are still together or not.

"Calm down, and I will talk to you later," Mr. Intelligence said and hung up.

After he hung up the phone, I called my youngest daughter. I was overtaken by how Jerry had used me, and I was weeping out of control. After explaining to her what was going on, she said the same thing the previous caller had said.

"Calm down, momma. Stop and think. I understand how and why you feel the way you do, and I probably would want to do the same thing, but you aren't in any physical shape to be fighting anyone."

"Pray, momma," she continued. No one knows, as well as you know by now, that God will fight your battles for you. Take a few minutes and calm down until God show you what to do."

I had already put Jerry in God's hands, and it just didn't appear that God was doing anything to him about all the things he had done and was still doing to me. I wanted to handle it myself.

On hearing this from my daughter, I began to take a deep breath and collect myself.

I called Jerry and informed him about the utility bill problem I was having, and as always, he had an excuse about why he had left the utility bill unpaid. He had no answer for me about why he hadn't told me that he had an apartment when I had left and had allowed him to take over my house--the house I was renting and had put so much into.

As usual, he was more concerned about himself than anything I was going through. He agreed to pay the old bill to have my utilities cut on in my new place.

Jerry paid the bill, but Mr. Intelligence just wouldn't let it go about how Jerry had done me. He was always making a joke about it on the phone or when we were together. I wasn't in any mood to see the funny side of how Jerry kept hurting me, in one way or another, over and over again.

My girlfriend and I drove down to the casino to have dinner the next night. Mr. Intelligence and his friend went along with us.

From the time I picked him and his friend up until the moment I dropped them back off at his place, Mr. Intelligence wouldn't stop making jokes about what Jerry had done to me.

He joked that he would get another place, and like Jerry, he wasn't going to tell me about it.

How childish of him. And I had now come to a place where I saw him in the same unfavorable light in which I saw Jerry. He, too, was not caring about my emotional well-being or how he was making me feel.

After I dropped him off, I was ready to drop him out of my life altogether. It also now angered my girlfriend, as she became aware of how he was treating me, even after he could see how displeased I was about the silly teasing he was doing.

My girlfriend and I talked as we drove home, but I was lost in the maze of all that was going on in my life.

After that night, I didn't speak to Mr. Intelligence or answer his call for a week.

It was getting harder and harder for me to take care of myself in this new place. Family and friends would sometimes call to check on me, but they all lived on the other side of town.

Jerry dropped by a few times and could see that I was having a hard time with the chemo and taking care of myself. I needed help, but everybody had their problems.

People would say, "Call me if you need me," but there was no one who I could call at midnight, at two or three in the morning or any of the times when I needed help. I know they meant well, but the truth was that they weren't in the position to help me the way I needed.

Having buried his wife, my son took his son and moved to Atlanta from Chicago to get some directions on what was next for him in life. He just couldn't deal with Chicago after my daughter-in-law's death, and I had no idea of what to tell him or how to help him.

There was no way any of us could help him because we weren't in his shoes. He allowed his newborn baby to stay in Chicago with her grandmother until he had gotten himself together and settled in his new city.

I was glad to hear he had decided to move on because I just wasn't in any shape to help him, myself. I prayed and prayed: *God, please help everyone in Chicago and help my baby (son)*. But everyone was praying for God to help me. My son had so much to deal with that he couldn't do anything for me. I just wanted him and his family to be alright.

Besides, God was helping me in more ways than I could see at the time.

Mother and her prayer-line had stepped up to take the number one place in my life. Even doing those midnight hours and those early morning hours when I was in so much pain. Many times, she would call and say, "Don't say a word, just listen to the prayer." I would just lay there crying as they prayed for me.

There were times when she connected me to others on the line that needed prayer to deal with cancer or needed prayer for a loved one who was dealing with it. I felt unworthy to pray for anyone, but I obeyed Mother and prayed anyway.

I now realized that I was being led more and more into a life that depended solely on God. Spending time with Mr. Intelligence was now becoming few and far between.

The chemo treatments were maker me sicker and weaker. Being bald had slowly become a part of me. I had worn wigs a lot before I got sick because I liked looking different, and I didn't care for the same look all the time. Now and then, before I got cancer and lost all of my hair, I would also try cutting my eyelashes. Being hairless had now become a part of this new look chemo had brought me.

Many of my loved ones and friends had voiced concern about me being in that house all alone. And I now could see why; I was fighting this invader with *all I had*, but all I had was becoming *not enough*.

The side effects of chemotherapy had started to be too much for me. When the urge to vomit came upon me, I would often find myself not having the physical strength to make it to the bathroom in time. When I regained strength and could sluggishly move about, I would have to tackle trying to clean myself up; this happened many times.

I would often try to force myself to eat, but many times it just wasn't happening. And when I could eat, the food would just come back up. After the food would come back up, I would hurt so bad that I would just forget about trying to eat.

My legs were so swollen; I would have to lift them with my hands to move them. My nails were turning black on my hands and my toes.

My finger bones hurt; my legs and arm bones also did.

Most of the side effects of having chemo treatments, which they warned me could happen, were now happening to me.

I found myself where it seemed impossible for me to live alone anymore and adequately take care of myself.

I was embarrassed by who I was and what I had become. I looked back over my life and asked God: *how did I get here? What had I done so bad that this was brought into my life?* But it appeared that God wasn't hearing me.

I began to cry, and then I asked myself: *Why would God help you--look at the way you have been living?*

But God Did! He did help me!

All of my life, I had allowed relationships with men to turn me from my goal of serving God and doing His will for my life. Here I was yet again, during the year in which my Heavenly Father was in the process of restoring me, dealing with issues from a relationship--with another man.

I was still talking to Mr. Intelligence, and I sometimes believed that he could be the man for me even though I knew he was not saved.

When it came to him, I couldn't think, and if I had been able to think, I didn't know what to think. I needed some help with what I was about to decide.

I went to this man that was in my life. Before I went, I rehearsed over and over in my head what I needed to say to him about what I needed from him. I finally stopped rehearsing the issue in my head and made the call.

As I attempted to explain what I needed from him, he was silent, but then he began to speak. He started to tell me that he just *couldn't keep going through this with me.* I was thinking: **What with me?**

He explained that I had brought him to tears more than once, and *he just wasn't going there anymore.* "The best thing for us to do is just go our separate ways," he said.

What is he talking about? I was puzzled and didn't understand why things were going the way they were going in the conversation.

In my mind, I asked, *what's really going on, Satan? It's got to be you. The moment I am ready to take this man at his word and say yes to him, he decides to get out of my life?*

Mr. Intelligence wouldn't let me say a word. He kept on telling me what he was going to do.

I couldn't speak. Something inside of me was asking God: *What is this?*

From that moment on, Mr. Intelligence turned into the man he had stated himself to be at the very beginning of our relationship. He was now keeping his creed which he had so often espoused: *Once a woman left him, he would not allow her back into his life.*

The thing was: *I wasn't trying to get out of his life.* I was calling to let him know how much I needed him to be more in mines.

How he had come to this conclusion from what I had just said over the phone was confusing to me. Nevertheless, it had come to this. The fling between He and I had finally ended.

I followed his instructions and retrieved my things at his house, and he came and picked up the stuff he had at mine.

I tried several more times to talk to him, but he would always say, "Nothing has changed." He still felt the same way, and he didn't want any more to do with me.

As puzzled as I was about how we had gotten to this place, I knew that this was the only place for him and me to be...**God had orchestrated this.**

I was now going home to God with the knowledge that: *Mr. Intelligence would have no place in his life for me* **<u>unless</u>** *I were outside of* **My Father's** *Will.*

I finally realized what was happening to us had nothing to do with Satan; This was God; he had provided a way of escape.

I Tim. 2:26 says, *"and that they (me) may recover themselves (myself) out of the snare of the devil, who are taken captive by him at his will." (KJV)*

God was using Mr. Intelligence's own law, which he had decreed: ***once a woman leaves him, he would never again have anything to do with her;*** to set me free from the adulterous bondage and ungodly soul tie I was entangled in for over eight months; *just like that;* ***it was over, and I was free!"***

OUT OF THE FRYING PAN AND INTO THE FIRE

<u>Now what?</u>

I was left with a lot of mixed feelings about what to do next. Yes, Mr. Intelligence was gone, but I was still dealing with the fact that my physical condition was getting worst. I still needed help in my life. The holidays were coming up, and I was trying to maintain my usual holiday spirit. I had moments where I was Burdened with concerns about how my son would make it without his wife. Then my thoughts would go to my grandsons, my new granddaughter, and then my daughter-in-law's family. Then I would focus on myself. It was hard, but I tried to get in a better mood by doing my holiday decorating. But there were times that I just couldn't shake it, and the thought of my baby (daughter-in-law) being gone would cause me to cry for days. Then that call came from the mother, and the prayer line that the sister in New Jersey had passed had broken my heart with grief.

As I mentioned earlier in my story, Mother had held back the news from me for a moment concerning this sister's death. She knew that this sister and I had become good friends who loved and prayed for each other, so she had put off telling me the news because she knew what it would do to me. When she told me, she held the phone, and she just listened to me cry. When I hung up the phone after hearing this news, I felt as though I was in a dark pit, and the pit was getting deeper and darker.

Everything is not going to be alright, I *(and the devil)* kept saying to myself. But there was no one to hear my cries. I was so overwhelmed and so alone.

When people called, attempting to comfort me, it didn't ease my loneliness, pains, and fears. I couldn't help but feel lost, no matter what people said or how people prayed for me. The different emotions that life had stacked upon me, and my problems appeared to worsen and worse. The worst of all was yet to come.

After one night of total despair, I picked up the phone and called Jerry. At that time, it had been months of no contact or conversation between us.

I explained to him that I wasn't sure why I called, but I needed him.

He could hear the despair in my voice. For the first time, he dropped what he was doing at work and came to see about me.

At the moment, nothing that had happened between us mattered. I was lost. But I had a husband. Despite what kind of husband he had been, he was still my husband.

I needed him. I needed his comfort and touch as I was trying to whole on to ***life*** itself.

No matter how much I believed that the LORD was there with me, I couldn't reach out and touch HIM, but I could touch Jerry.

Jerry's being there with me brought on all kinds of problems for him. He was caught now between what was "*blessed and **true***" and the "*cursed lie*" he had been living with this woman. In the eyes of God, Jerry is still mine.

I was now about to enter into a whole new level of pain and loneliness.

It was as if for the first time in our lives, Jerry could see what he had done to me. As he tried to step up to the plate and do the right thing for me, it was as though the devil stepped up his game by declaring open war on the both of us.

According to His Way, it wasn't going to be a battle easy for me to win because I had come back to God and would have to fight fair. I was far too complacent and unacknowledged about how dirty the devil can play.

I was still ignorant about people. That little idea I had in my head that most people have some morals was about to be proven false and blatantly incorrect.

Jerry tried to be there for me, but he was very confused about how he would handle being with *his woman* and *being my husband at the same time.*

I needed him, yet in all the many ways I needed him, I just couldn't settle for having only part of him. He would go back and forth, giving the other woman a portion of him and me the other part. She had bewitched his soul, and even though he didn't realize it, he was more afraid of her than he was of God.

I still wanted my husband. Through my experiences, I realized that God doesn't always do what you ask or believe for Him to do. My baby was dead, my prayer sister was dead, every time I went for chemo treatments, there would be someone on the right side of me who had passed, and then someone on the left side of me was gone.

How did I know that I wasn't next? How? I didn't want to die alone. I just didn't want to die alone. Jerry was my husband. A husband's place was beside his wife. If it had been him in my stead, I would have been there for him; by his side.

But his other woman wasn't about to just sit back and let that happen. She had no concern for the fact that I was ill and that I was the man's wife. She had seduced Jerry into her bed and her life. The only thing that mattered to her was how to keep him there. She made it plain that what she had to do to keep him, she was going to do it—no matter whether it was the will of God or not.

God was my only defense. All I had was God, and without Him, I knew I couldn't fight the battle.

I didn't know whether this invader of cancer was going to allow me to live long enough to have any other man in my life. For now, Jerry was my husband, and she and no one else could change that.

Once family, friends, and church members realized that I was back with my husband, they began to ask me what I was doing to myself by trying to whole on to him.

Everyone kept warning me that I had too much to deal with already to allow myself to get back involved with the mayhem which Jerry and this woman had put me through.

Mother and the prayer-line warriors were concerned about what would happen in my life by taking him back. But no one understood how I felt. How could they? It wasn't them dealing with this cancer, and I didn't want to be alone. It wasn't them, but me. So how could they say what they would or wouldn't do? How could they tell me that getting back with Jerry wasn't best for me? How could they know what was best?

My family and friends weren't there when the chemo would make me so sick that I wasn't able to bathe or clean myself up. They were not there when the radiation burned me so; that the flesh would fall from my bones.

No one was there when a chemo patient next to me during one treatment was gone when I went back for my next treatment. They weren't there, God, they weren't there.

I needed Jerry. I needed someone, and there was no other person there.

I didn't care about what Jerry's other woman thought. I didn't care how she felt. She shouldn't have fallen in love with my husband. She should at least have waited until there was a divorce to grab him. But she didn't, and I was tired of putting everyone else's feelings, needs, and wants before my own.

She had planned a trip to New Orleans during the Thanksgiving holiday, and he had carried me through emotional hell about whether he would go with her or not. It was clear to me that she was doing everything in her power to keep my husband in her life. It was becoming evident to me that he wanted to keep getting all that she was providing.

And he didn't want to let her go either.

My friends were worried sick about what they saw happening to be because of this woman.

However, my heart could *only hear* this silent fear that was in the back of my mind, "I don't want to die alone..." So, the nightmare continued.

After he returned from the trip with her, he came over the next night to see me. I was a mess. I could no longer take this emotional pain Jerry kept putting me through, even if I had to die alone. It was just too much. So I started pushing him back out the door as I scolded him with a battery of words. I just wanted to get him out of my life for good.

I can't deal with you and her. Make a choice; either stay with me or go back to her. Make a choice, now. Make a choice; I cried and screamed!

He took hold of my hands to stop me from pushing him out of the door. "I will stay," he said. I stopped and just looked at him. "I will stay here with you."

I fell apart, crying as he held me in his arms. "I don't know how to do this," he said. "All hell is going to break loose, but I will stay with you. I can't keep hurting you this way, Joann."

I was so soaked in sweat and emotionally drained that I couldn't stand on my feet anymore. He told me just to lie down, as he laid there beside me, I fell asleep.

When the next morning came, Jerry left and went to work. We both knew that all of hell was about to come against us. The two of us being together as **God-willed**; was not on the devil's list or in his plans for us.

Satan wasn't going to sit back and allow us to come together and live happily ever after, like in the fairy tales. *Oh No!* That was just not going to happen.

I had been Satan's *captive in sin*, but now, I had gotten away and was pursuing **God** and **His Will** for my life. The devil didn't like this.

I was no longer in the enemy camp doing my own thing. I had not only come back to God, but I was in a place now where I had never been before...in **God's perfect will.**

God had totally delivered me. The sex demon was now gone. The fact that I felt the need for my husband had nothing to do with sex. I was a new woman, and I just wanted never to fail my Father,

Lord, and Savior again. I knew I would never fail HIM again in my sex life, no matter if Jerry stayed in my life or not.

Since I had gone to a new place in my spiritual walk with God--a place of total surrender; the only thing left for the devil to do was to use my husband and this woman to try to destroy me, while I was physically at my weakest point in life.

Just as Jerry and I had predicted, all hell broke loose. Jerry didn't go back to her house at all that week. I would wash his work clothes at night, and he would wear them again the next day.

She was showing up at his job or calling his workplace every minute. She would stalk him and would try to jump him whenever she could get close enough.

Since the prayer line was such an essential part of my life, Jerry couldn't help but listen when I was on the line.

One morning as the prayer partners were praying for the two of us, Jerry took the phone and asked if they would please pray for him. "I really need it," he said.

One of the prayer line mothers from Oklahoma replied and told him that she would, and from that day until now, she has never stopped asking God to save his soul and do work for him.

The weekend came, and *the hell* escalated to another level. Jerry was now talking to his supposed ex-lover on the phone constantly. I would mostly just sit back and listen, not knowing what to do.

Jerry was in a mess, and he was tactfully trying to deal with it, but the woman wouldn't let up. She refused to give him a way out.

We went to visit his family in Mississippi that Saturday to get out of town for a moment. His family was confused, seeing Jerry and me together. His girlfriend was ringing the phone, calling his family, trying to make contact with him. This was weird and *out of place*, I thought to myself.

I wasn't feeling well at all when we made it back into town, but I didn't say much. Jerry just turned his phone off, and we talked for a moment about the load and stress we were under because of what was going on.

Jerry, being exhausted, fell asleep but being in pain, I just prayed to God. The following day we got ready for church.

That next day, Jerry went to church with me at this new Ministry I had started attending. While we were there, the **Spirit** moved so heavily, both Jerry and I could feel it in our midst. After services ended, we were trying to go when someone called me. Jerry waited at the door for me. While he was waiting, one of the ministers introduced himself and began to talk with him.

Then, this minister's wife, who is also a minister, began telling him what the **LORD** had given her to say. Everything she said was just what he was going through, and she also told him what he had to do. We both were amazed how The **LORD** spoke to him, assuring him that he was in the right place and was now doing the right thing.

As we started for the car, the pastor saw us through the church hallway's window, called out to us. We both stopped, and I told the pastor who he was. But the pastor already knew. He had seen him during the service. For a brief moment, everything that day was going well, but it wasn't going to last for long.

Sticking with our plans, we now made our way to the church where we both had once attended. Everyone there seemed confused to see us walk in together.

There were a lot of smiles from different members.

Before Jerry and I could really get seated, I looked back and saw Jerry's girlfriend coming in the door. She came up to Jerry and asked could she speak with him.

Jerry looked at me and told me to stay right there and that he would be back. I sat back down and tried to do what he said, but the two of them were arguing quite loudly, and people could hear it from the inside of the church.

I got up and went out to where they were. Some of the sisters came out right behind me. Several of the deacons were out there also, and one of them had already called the police.

When I got to the door, I could see that she was pulling on his clothes as he tried to get her to just go back to her van. She said something about cutting him, and I started to go where the two of them were, but someone caught one of my arms, and another person grasped the other.

"No, sister," they both start saying. "No! You can't allow her to take you to as low of a place as she just took herself." "What do you mean no, that's my husband, and this woman is talking about cutting him. If she's low enough to disrespect our church, disrespect the service, and disrespect him and me, then cutting him would not be beneath her either."

"But this is beneath you. And who are you, pastor?" the voice continued with conviction. Don't let her take you there. It's not what God wants you to do", they both said. "Just come back inside and let him handle it.

I calmed myself down and took their advice, but this was not what I wanted to do.

Jerry headed back toward the church, but she came at him again, trying to fight him. I went outside the door again, watching the both of them.

Someone mentioned calling the police, and she started heading back to her van. As she walked back towards the van, she turned around, looked at me, and asked: "What do you have to say?"

I didn't say anything. Everything in me was saying: *Don't let her cause you to dishonor God and his House.* So, I just looked at her. Then she said, "I didn't think you had anything to say." Again, a small voice within me spoke and said, *don't let her cause you to do anything that will make it look like you don't trust ME.*

I went back inside and stood looking at Jerry while others in the room were making comments about what had just happened. *If she would do something like that, she will do anything*, one deacon said. Then another commented: that *type of woman is crazy, and you can't turn your back on her, brother*. I watched Jerry as one remark after another was spoken to him, but none of the statements were based on **God's Word** of **His** way of doing things. Not one comment had anything to do with encouraging him or telling him he should leave that woman alone... pray for her and cleave to his wife.

I never opened my mouth; I just kept watching him. When the police came and began to take his statement, I listened close to what he had to say.

He answered all their questions. Then they told him what to do the following day at the courthouse. As we drove home from the church, Jerry couldn't stop talking about how this woman had had the nerves to jump on him and say she would cut him.

We didn't go home, but we went to my daughter's house. When we got over to my daughter's house, we realized that she was trailing a few cars behind us in her van. This made him uneasy. He kept saying, "I just don't want to go to jail dealing with this woman, but I just might have to hurt her to keep her from hurting me."

When we did get home, he got on the phone and talked to his oldest daughter and told her about what had happened at the church.

By hearing what he was saying to his daughter, I realize this woman had Jerry just where she wanted him. He was upset and afraid that this woman would cause him to do something crazy, and he would end up in jail. She had him just where she wanted. He was intimidated and fearful of going to jail.

I knew at that moment that everything was about to change. I wasn't the kind of woman who would intentionally do something to disgrace Jerry or God. The fact that I wasn't that type of woman would be ***my loss*** in this fight.

We went downtown to the police station the following day. Jerry was trying to fill out his paperwork and restraining order discretely. I wouldn't see the information he was writing, especially the woman's phone number and address. When he realized that I knew what he was doing, he said to me, "I won't tell her where you stay, and I don't want you to know where she lives either."

I thought to myself, *but you told me just a few days ago that she had called some friend of hers who works at the light company and had gotten my address and that she had been driving back and forth in front of my house, watching to see when you would be here.*

I reminded him of this. *She already knows where I stay;* I said, why don't you want me to know where she lives? He just said, "I don't want any more problems than there already are." We finished at the courthouse, and Jerry left for work.

At work that day, she showed up at his job, and the fight continued. By this time, everyone in my life had heard about what happened at church. Now I was being battered from every side about how I didn't need all this drama in my life. *You need to just stay focus on yourself, don't let them do this to you, Joann.* But I wasn't letting anybody do anything; they were just doing it. If God wasn't stopping them, what in the world could I do?

Trying to whole on to him is going to cause you just to suffer more. Just let him go, Joann, just let him go; the voices continued.

How? How was I just going to let him go? No one could answer that question, and I sure didn't have an answer. I will have nothing; *if I let him go, I will have no one*, I argued. "But you really don't have anyone anyway," one of my friends said. "He's not yours. He may be your husband, but he's not going to leave that other woman."

"I am sorry to say this to you, Joann, but he has never really loved you like a man should love a wife. Your marriage to him was really all about your love for him, and never was it about him loving you. Let it go. Please let it go. The devil is just using them to try to kill you. Let it go, please", my girlfriend pleaded.

In my mind, I began to say to her; *but I don't want to die alone, I don't want to die alone.* I just couldn't let those words come out of my mouth. I just couldn't. So I just cried; as I hung up the phone.

The next few weeks with him were filled with nothing but hell for me. Every night Jerry got off from work, he was coming home later and later, but each night he had an excuse.

After about two weeks of him disrespecting me in this manner, I realized the situation was getting worse and worse, and I couldn't whole my head up anymore.

The Christmas holiday was approaching, and she was using the foster kids, shopping, her money, and everything she could to get Jerry back.

I remember telling God; *I have only you. And Jerry isn't interested in either of us at this time.*

Once, he made it home that night after leaving work and doing **whatever** it was after 11 p.m. We were supposed to be going to Atlanta. I had been trying to pack our things for the trip. He had brought a few of his things to my place, but she was holding on to most of his stuff, so they both would have an excuse for him to keep coming over to her place.

He came home that night as though he had done nothing wrong. It seemed that the more he made it a habit to go to her place before coming home to me, the easier it got for him to do. He just came in, washed his hands, and got his food. He then sat down in front of the television and started eating. "What time do you want to leave tomorrow," he asked? As I stood in the doorway, I remember looking down on him as he was eating and saying; *God sees what the two of you are doing, Jerry, and one day, both of you will pay for it.*

(I Peter 3:12) states, *"For the eyes of the Lord are on the righteous, and his ears are open to their prayers. But the face of the Lord is against those who do evil."*

(I Chronicles 16:9) reads, *"For the eyes of the LORD run to and fro throughout the whole earth, to show Himself strong on behalf of those whose heart is loyal to Him."* Jerry looked at me as I stood there in the doorway and uttered,

"Yeah, I know."

The Christmas holiday had come, and we all were going to Atlanta to spend it with my son. Jerry had agreed to go because most of his family would be in the Atlanta area for the holiday. He left that morning to take care of something at work, but I knew that he was going by to see her before he left. She had been calling all morning, as usual.

We waited what seemed like forever for him to come back so we could leave. My daughter was growing angrier and angrier at me because she knew where he was and felt that we should let him just stay where he wanted to be.

I knew she was right, and as we started to load up the cars to leave, Jerry drove up. The whole time we were in Atlanta, Georgia, he was on the phone with his girlfriend in Memphis. I had taken my mother with us, who has dementia. I had my hands full. It was the worst Christmas I've ever had. Jerry used my son's car and found his family that Saturday, and while he was gone, I decided that it was best if we just left and returned to Memphis.

My mother and I were exhausted and too tired to do anything but go back home to Memphis. I wanted to get back home (ASAP) before losing all of my strength and just collapsed. We made it back on Sunday, in the early morning hours. I asked Jerry was he going to church, and he said, "No." I had made plains to meet one of my friends that day after church services, so I forced myself to go.

After church service, something just wasn't quite right in my Spirit. While I was in church, I tried with all I had to stay focused on God, but my physical and emotional pain was overshadowing everything. *How much longer are you going to put up with this, Joann; I asked myself.*

I knew Jerry was probably with this woman by now, and I wasn't prepared to keep hurting myself.

LORD, I just don't know what to do. In my Spirit, I heard a voice saying; you have allowed them to take you low enough, don't go any lower, Joann. No More. No matter what happens to you...**No more.**"

I went back to the house and gathered the few things that Jerry still had there. He didn't know it, but I knew where she lived. I told myself: if you go there and he's there, it's time to end this.

I went there, and before I could turn the corner, I saw that his truck was parked in front of her house. I had no idea that both of my daughters were at a friend's house just up the street. So when I pulled up in front of the woman's door and began to throw all of his things in the back of his truck, they saw me. I was acting like ***another woman—*** what I was doing was out of character for me as a Christian lady.

Before I could finish throwing all of his things out of my car and into his truck, my daughters pulled up in a car in front of me. My oldest daughter started talking to me, amazed at what I was doing. Seeing their mother doing what she was doing--they knew I was acting out of character.

My youngest daughter was ready to do whatever it took to make sure no one touched her mother. She was prepared to fight with me if it came down to it. She was always a lot to handle.

I became so embarrassed for my daughters to see me acting this way that I hurriedly finished what I was doing and drove off. *What am I doing, LORD? Where has this man taken me to?*

Once Jerry and his woman noticed inside the house what was going on, the two came out. *My daughters told me this later.*

A few words were exchanged between Jerry and my daughters before my girls drove off.

He tried calling me to apologize and explain his actions. But in the end, he used what I had done only as an excuse to get back under his girlfriend's roof. Now it was my fault that he had to go back to her. This whole thing with the two of them had literally drained me of my strength.

The pastor of the church I was visiting called to check on me because he had offered to pray and talk to Jerry; he wanted God to give us clear directions.

When I told him about what had happened between Jerry and me, I never will forget how I felt upon hearing his response.

"Sister, how could you let them take you so low that you found yourself out in the street throwing his clothes in front of her door? This woman isn't making him do anything. He has given her the right to do the things she is doing. It's not her. He's going along with it because that's where he wants to be. Can't you see that?"

Yes, I answered, and then I just listened while he prayed for me.

This is very difficult to write about, re-living all this pain. I pray that God gives me what I need to finish this book as HE has promised me he would do. This book will fall into the hands of others who have faced pain or who are facing similar pain or even greater adversity and hardships. Please, LORD, shield their hearts. Wrap their minds in You Holy Ghost so that they may realize that you are there, and you will never leave them alone to face any adversity in life.

LORD, *I'm not asking you to move this mountain (my enemies) ...I realize that people will be people. And when people don't fear and reverence You, they will do anything to themselves and others. Lord, knowing through your* **Word** *those trials and tribulations give us* <u>strength and patience</u> **(Romans 5:1-5)**, *I'm praying and asking You* **LORD regarding** *all of my mountains: Please, give me the strength to climb them.*

In Jesus' holy and precious Name, Amen.

Readers, I would like every one of you to remember what I am now about to say; **please remember:** *There is a price to pay for being a minister or being a born-again son or daughter of God; for to whom much is given, much is required. However,* **no one** *is exempt from trouble, not even the* **sinner.** *Job said that* **every man** *born of a woman would exist in* <u>this physical body and on this earth</u> *for only a few days, and those days would be filled with trouble.*

Trials abound in the **Ministry** and the lives of all *born-again believers. Many are the affliction of the righteous, but the Lord will deliver him from them all.*

II Corinthian 4: 11 reminds and prepares us for trouble: *"We are troubled on every side, yet not distressed; we are perplexed, but not in despair; Persecuted, but not forsaken; cast down, but not destroyed; Always bearing about in the body the dying of the Lord Jesus, that the life also of Jesus might be made manifest in our body. For we which live are always delivered unto death for Jesus' sake, that the life also of Jesus might be made manifest in our mortal flesh."*

Thank You, LORD, for finding me worthy to be your daughter, even after all the wrong I'm revealing in this book that I've done...Thanks for letting me represent YOU: as a Minister and child of the Almighty God!

GOING BEYOND MY ABILITY

Thank You, LORD! The holidays were over, and the radiation and chemo were taking a toll on my body. Jerry was still, sometimes calling me, and we were still going back and forth about *whom done who wrong.*

I really wasn't able to do for myself, but being who I was, I wasn't going to let anyone know.

I was having a hard time paying bills and getting in and out of stores to shop for my personal needs. A social worker told me about a program that would help me with my housework and my health needs which I immediately signed up for.

This nursing service helped me twice a week, but I wouldn't allow them to do anything personal. I had lost mostly everything, but I wasn't about to lose my dignity too. So, I struggled to take care of bathing and cleaning myself. It was becoming clearer and clearer by the minute that I wouldn't be able to keep this up. I couldn't survive too much longer, living by myself and trying to make it on my own.

I cried night and day with tears that only heaven could witness because, with everyone else, I wasn't going to reveal or show my aching heart. I was at rock bottom, but I was about to find out that rock bottom has another bottom underneath it. In my despair, I kept reaching out for Jerry, but he kept pushing me further and further away.

"You're acting just like she said you would," was the *mantra* Jerry mouthed to me every time I did or said something to him. I gave up again and again on trying to get Jerry; to still play a part in my life. But with every *downward spiral* with my health, I would reach out for him again. Hours were spent with me telling Jerry about the ungodly situation he was in and encouraging him that he should seek God for a way out. Despite all he had done to me, I still wanted and prayed that he might be the **man of valor** I believed he could be in God.

Every time we would converse, Jerry would conclude that everything wrong that he was now doing was because of me.

One Monday morning, I went by my youngest daughter's house, and just like that, she and I were in this heated argument. I don't even remember what it was about. But it drove me into deeper despair.

Feeling brokenness in every part of my life, I called my son. He was very forward with me and told me: "You just can't live like this anymore, momma."

"Momma, I can't keep running back and forward trying to see about you. What you need to do now is to allow me just to come and get you. You will have to stay with me until you are better and can take care of yourself.

My son had already been through so much. I didn't want him to have to re-live what he had gone through with his wife by watching me go through the same things that she had faithfully endured.

My son believed that by being in Atlanta with him, he would be more able to help me because he could then personally see and know what to do for me. I couldn't fight anymore, so once again, I gave up having my place to soon move to Georgia to live with my son.

I sold what I could of my possessions and put the rest in storage. I then moved in temporarily with my sister, who lived in the same city where I lived. She had an extra bedroom, and she prepared it for me. Once again, I was back at her place; until I could finish the radiation treatments before moving to Atlanta.

I was on my 25th treatment when my flesh began sticking to everything I touched. I was in so much pain that I would just sit and rock while crying vehemently. My sister came into the kitchen one day and found me like this. She put her arms around me and began to cry with me. "I wish there were something I could do," she said. Then she began to pray for me.

I had six more treatments. Because of the severity of my cancers when they had found them, I was told I would have to have all the chemo treatments available. I screamed out so with pain during that 26th treatment; the doctor had to put me in the hospital and start morphine.

I spent the next eight days in the hospital. My pastor and wife from the ministry that Jerry and I attended together and had held positions at came to see me. The pastor and wife from the current church I had become involved with came to see me, also.

Phone calls from family, friends, and church members were coming at all times of the day and night.

When Jerry found out I was in the hospital, he called to let me know that he wished he could see me but being in the situation he was in; *it just wasn't possible.*

I was in so much pain; whatever Jerry said or did, didn't matter anymore. All I wanted was for God to relieve my pain.

In constant prayer, mother and the prayer line were on duty, only stopping to inform me that God **said I shall live and not die**. Prayers were going on **ever the more** on my behalf. *Someone was praying for me and had me on their mind, and took a little time to pray for me.*

I now know that even when it seemed as though I was alone, I wasn't. Many people were there for me and had my back through prayer. After I got out of the hospital, it was time to prepare my things and move to Atlanta. The last thing I wanted was to put myself off on my son, but I had no other choice at the time. For the first four to six months after moving there, it became a routine trip to drive back to Memphis for the medical treatments I needed. This was because it took that long for me to get health care started in Atlanta. I loved the drive from Atlanta to Memphis. I often felt too weak and exhausted to make the trip, but I wasn't about to let anyone know it. These trips became a haven for me. I had always loved being out on the open road. The drives to Memphis mostly took place between the hours of 8 p.m. and 6 a.m.

I was forever being warned about being out on the road by myself, but I wasn't by myself. The Holy Spirit always showed Himself mighty and strong while I was behind the wheel. There were times where I would have to pull over and just take a break.

Many times, as I made the trip from Atlanta to Memphis, I would be on my cell phone, talking to different people for hours and hours, and miles and miles.

One of the greatest moments during those drives was when I would call the prayer line while on the road. Mother and different partners would talk and pray for me to the end of my journey.

"Where are you now?" they would ask. It was beautiful how they would laugh and talk with me. Different ones would often tell about their road trips and how they agreed with me that there was something remarkable about going from place to place and seeing diverse landscapes. We talked about how God was this great artist, and He had placed his signature in the earth, in so many different places, and so many different ways. I loved it! I loved it: The trees, the grass, the first blooming of the leaves in the spring, and then--nature's colors turning red and brown in the autumn. I was free on the highway of life, and there was no one standing between me and the **LORD!** I would be in physical pain many times, but I would persevere and keep moving down the road.

The Holy Spirit would come in through my music, and I would sing as the words of the song would enter my heart and reverberate through my lips. Over and over, I would get caught up in the rhythms, the beats, and with every different note and tone. As I would saturate myself in the warmth of the music, before I knew anything, the pain would be gone.

Sometimes I would get so caught up in the music and the songs of praise on the c.d. that was playing that I would stop my car for a moment, and I would stand outside my car and dance with joy.

Often truckers or other drivers on the dark road would hunk their horns and shout out their windows at me as they watched me rejoice in the LORD. I would get so off-into my music that when I reached my destiny, and the song hadn't finished, I would just sit there in the car until the song was ended, saturated in the warmth of the Spirit of God. *I was in the zone and in the presence of God.*

While making these night trips in my little red car, sometimes I cried, shouted, groaned in pain, or laughed, but never once did I give up or quit.

And the Holy Spirit would always meet me there, on the road. I loved driving. And out of all the different things I lost during this time of adversity, God never allowed me to lose my ability to drive.

It was nothing but the "Holy Ghost" that kept me with that gift...I began to have problems with my right hand and arm due to the limp nodes that had been taken from underneath my arm, yet my driving skills were unhampered. When I could no longer use my right arm, I could still use my left one. **Isn't that like God!** HE always makes a way. It wasn't until I lost some of the strength in my right arm and could no longer use it effectively; I then realized that I had driven with my left hand for most of my life anyway. God had prepared me for this time in my life long before it ever came. **Praise is to You, God!** I don't think I could have made it through all the hardships during my illness if I hadn't been able to drive.

Driving kept me in control of my life. It kept me from just lying down and dying. I had no control over all the bad things that were happening to me. But the Holy Ghost kept me with the ability to drive in and out of different cities and states, also out of many problems and heartaches. I kept driving and moving down the road of life.

After several months of living in Georgia, my health coverage there came into effect. Now, I would not have to drive back and forward so much to Tennessee.

After completing my chemo and radiation treatments, my next big step was reconstructive surgery. I was ready for this next step. God once again hooked me up with one of the best doctors in the field. She and her staff were wonderful to me.

Since I wasn't traveling so often now, I began to look for a place to worship in Atlanta. I prayed for the Holy Spirit to lead me where to go. The area that my son lived in the city, I didn't care for.

I really didn't know why; I just didn't. I never saw a lot of black people in that area. Nevertheless, I would always come across this little church, so one Wednesday night, I visited it.

The ministry warmly welcomed me. There weren't many members there, but those who were there seemed genuine and serious about their faith and God. Those months of being on the road by myself had taken me to the place where I was falling madly in love with the LORD. So when I saw how the members expressed that same type of love for HIM, I felt that this would be the place for me-- until the Holy Spirit led me on.

I began to enjoy right away the pastor's style of teaching and leading God's people. It was clear after just a short time that he and his wife were good examples of what a married couple should be in the Lord. He was steadfast in his beliefs and taught the subject of marriage very strongly. It was overwhelming for me, but I felt that this was what I needed. So, I decided to stay; I had found a home.

They had Monday night prayer meetings. So I began to attend them also. I wasn't sure if God would allow me to go back home to Memphis or stay in Atlanta, so I didn't join this church at the time.

I had never before witnessed such a strong stance on men being the head of their marriage and home.

I had been saved since 1985, but I had to admit that I couldn't ever remember being taught with such conviction about marriage, the way it was coming forth in this ministry.

The more I sat and listened, the more I was educated about what it took to be a good wife. The Holy Spirit spoke to me and told me that I was about to learn what it meant to be a "wife" in the LORD...I was blown away.

The pastor would teach the men about their roles as godly men and their roles as the head of their household; he would deal with them about it.

The men in that ministry were taking their role as heads in the church in a way that I had never really witnessed in other ministries. They were serious and united with their pastors in pursuing the calling of who the Lord had made them be. I began to feel things within me changing.

The first lady and most of the women seemed to understand who they were in their marriages and properly behave themselves as women of God.

Under this ministry, I began to feel safe and protected by the men.

The people there who spoke up and openly about marriage difference issues were open, bold, and firm. The wives seemed to be willing to follow their pastor's instructions in dealing with their husbands, who were not in the church and unsaved at the time.

These women were crying out, seeking God for what they needed to be the type of "wife" he had called for them to be. That was something I hadn't done with my marriages, neither did I know how to do it *until I met these women*. I could hear, within my spirit, the Holy Spirit speaking to me, saying, "There is nothing wrong, Joann, about wanting to be a **_wife_** because you never really knew how to be one. If you don't know how to be a wife to me, how will you ever know how to be one to a man?"

I repented to God for what I had done and how I had done things my way in my marriages and life. I had never allowed God to be _everything_ to me. I had accused Jerry of doing the same things with women, which I was guilty of with men. *I had gone from man to man my entire life.*

Throughout my life, I had had no example of what a real man was, and all the men that I had married had had no good examples of being real men or godly husbands.

Under this ministry, I realized that I had never married for the right reasons before.

I started to really understand and see the many things that I had done wrong in Jerry and my marriage. From the very beginning, we didn't marry for the right reason or right way.

We married because we wanted to, and not because it was God's will for us.

I knew when I met Jerry that God had a call on his life. I had tried to help him to see it. But what I was learning now was that I had done it in the wrong way and for the wrong reasons. I fell deeply in love with the man, and I wouldn't give him up. Had I been willing to give him up to God, maybe things could have turned out differently.

Jerry didn't have to marry any of the other women that had come in and out of his life--to be with them. I came into his life with *changes and orders* of what he had to do and be. But he wasn't mine; he was God's. By not waiting and allowing God to perform the changes that Jerry needed in his life, I failed.

Through this disciplined and godly ministry, the **Holy Spirit** was convicting my spirit and was constantly doing work on me.

Psalms 51-17 reads, *"The sacrifices of God are a broken spirit, a broken and a contrite heart"* ...

Psalms 34:18 proclaims, *"The Lord is near to those who have a broken heart and saves such as have a contrite spirit."* (This refers to those who are crushed and broken in spirit and are willing to surrender their all to HIM totally).

The things I was learning about marriage were overwhelming to me. As I sat there in the congregation and reminisced of all the pain and disappointment, I had endured regarding how I had to handle my marriages- inwardly, I began to weep with sorrow.

The autumn was coming. In October, my reconstruction surgery had been scheduled. Due to my son's busy schedule and my grandson being in daycare, I would have to be dropped off to face the surgery alone, and my son would have to come back later to get me.

Being left to face surgery alone wasn't new to me. The surgery was a major one, and I awakened, this time, to the most pain I had ever faced after a surgery.

I had made it through the surgery and was in my room when something started going wrong. I was fading in and out, and it appeared that I couldn't control my limbs' movements. I could hear different voices saying something about a code (code blue), and then my ability to hear started fading.

Ms. Swims, Ms. Swims. The doctor was calling out, instructing me to keep my eyes on her. But keeping my eyes open at all was impossible to do. Now everyone in the room was calling out my name. I could see people running in and out of the room. Something was wrong, but I didn't know what.

I could feel myself fading out, and there was nothing I could do about it. I awakened hours later, with all kinds of machines attached to me. As I looked up, I noticed a line that was carrying blood to my vein. **What happened?** I tried to ask, but my speech was slurred and dragged as I talked. The doctor said, "We lost you for a moment, Mrs. Swims, but we have everything in control now. You had a sudden blood drop, and we had to give you more blood.

Until your blood level is back where it needs to be, we will keep giving you blood."

I thanked the Lord as I started to go out again under the medication. From that day on, it was disappointment after disappointment regarding issues with my reconstructed surgery.

The cut where they had removed the skin on my stomach, which was used to provide the flesh needed to reconstruct the *removed flesh*, was healing. But the areas where the flesh had been applied to weren't healing well at all. It appeared that I still had so much radiation in that part of my body that it was eating away at the new flesh that had been placed there. This opened up a whole different problem. And more complications would soon develop.

After the surgery and stay in the hospital, I was sent home with a nursing service assigned to come and help me with what was becoming a very bad wound. All hope of having a breast there was fading away fast.

This was unbearable! The only reason why I faced the removal of that breast was because of the hope that another one could be constructed there.

Why God? Why so much pain? I would listen to people who would try to make me feel better about what was happening to me. But it just didn't work. The flesh in my breast area was turning black and hard. My surgeon was explaining that the flesh that was dying would have to be removed.

This was going to be the fourth surgery I would have to have, and we all knew that there was going to have to be more in the future. All I could do now was cry.

Everyone was trying to help me through this with encouraging words and prayer, but nothing helped.

November the 12th came, and once again, I was in surgery.

After the surgery, I looked at my body, and there were holes in my chest. You could see the lining of my ribs through one of them.

Holes, God, I got spots in my chest. I was trying to keep my composure because I didn't want my son to worry about me. I would lie in my bed with the door closed and place a pillow over my mouth so no one could hear me crying. I was in so much agony and pain. And I had now been reduced to a fraction of a woman. I got sick and tired of hearing people saying that I shouldn't worry about it: *The man that will come into your life will want you for who you are, whether you have a breast there or not.*

It wasn't about whether a man would ever want me again; it was about me. I was less than whole now, and I had believed that God would make me complete again. Nothing that I had believed for in my life was happening. **NOTHING.**

If the reconstructive surgery had worked, I wouldn't be going through this; I silently voiced within. Why Go, Why?

I would have to see a wound doctor; nothing else could be done until the wound in my chest was healed. Whenever the nursing service would come and clean that wound out, I would be overcome with embarrassment and shame. I wouldn't allow my son to help me; I didn't want him to see me that way. There were times when I didn't have enough <u>strength</u> or <u>heart</u> to look at my chest.

While I was at this new church, I met this brother. He and I started talking one day during fellowship after one of their conventions. We had a lot in common, but we mostly had in common our love for God.

I had been asking God for help. I was hoping for someone to love me, but this wasn't the type of love I had asked for. This was brotherly love, and this brother, through God's grace and Spirit, became a rock and shield for me.

Another thing we had in common was that; we both had been deeply hurt by the people we loved. We both had gotten into bad relationships because we didn't consult God. And we both were suffering pain due to it. I thanked God for bringing this brother into my life.

It took a little time, but this man had now become an example to me of what a godly man should be. He was a man who still had many things to learn from God, but he was a man who loved the Lord, so much so that he was willing to be honest about his shortcomings in the Lord. I was able to contact his ex-wife, and we were all happy about the way he was growing in the Lord.

I had filed for my divorce before I left Memphis, but Jerry just wouldn't do what was needed to be done for the divorce to go through. In the beginning, he talked about helping me financially every two weeks. I didn't think that this was too much since I had helped him with his schooling. It took me months of prompting and encouraging Jerry before he would go and get the education, he needed to receive fair pay for the work he did.

As I stated, Jerry was a faithful worker. He had worked with heating and air and had done electrical work for years on his jobs. It just didn't seem right to me for him not to be paid sufficiently for his work. After trying to get him to get the education he needed so people could pay him properly for the type of work he did, I took it upon myself to go to the school and get the information and papers he needed. And then I brought them to him to fill out to apply for school.

I was working two jobs at the time. And I paid all the bills at home so he could focus only on paying for his classes and books. Once he got started, he loved it and took advanced courses in his employment field.

Because I had done so much for my husband in the past, I didn't think that it was improper for him to help me out financially now. He did begin to help me financially, but he kept *going down* on the amount of money he would send me each pay period. I was now preoccupied with going through the treatments to heal my body, so I wasn't able to keep fighting Jerry about the financial support he had agreed to give me routinely. But I loved him and was praying for him as my husband, even though he lived as some other woman's husband. I couldn't answer for Jerry to God, but I would have to answer God for my conduct.

Until the Lord allowed the divorce to come through, I followed the pastor's instructions, given to women with unsaved husbands. It didn't seem like it mattered at that point to no one; except God and me.

I would not ever let God down again, so I did the things that would allow me to draw nigh and get closer to the **LORD.** The Holy Spirit was instructing me to keep doing all I had learned about being a wife. He told me that Jerry was the head. And as the head, Jerry would be the one **HE** would use to make the final decision in our marriage.

The spirit of God informed me that Jerry would not know this, but I would. God would orchestrate the decisions he would make. ***Be patient and wait my child; was God's command to me.***

I took a moment to reminisce about the different men I had placed in headship over my life. Never once did I submit or allow even one of them to be the head over me and adequately fulfill that role.

Whether you understand this or not, ladies, the man is the head. Regardless of what he's doing or not doing, the man is the **Head**. God holds us accountable for who we place over us or who, we as women, vow to let be head over us, whether they are *saved or not*.

When a woman enters marriage without praying or given thought to whom they're placing over their lives as her headship, and the one she will honor and obey for the rest of her life—she's making a big decision.

Once a woman makes that vow of marriage, God expects her to live up to it by humbling herself to her husband. The issue of marriage is so important to God that He likens it and compares it to Christ being married to the church. The angel in **Revelations 21:9b** gestured to John: *"...Come, and I will show you the bride, the Lamb's wife."* Christ, Himself is the Lamb, and the church is his bride.

The definition of a vow is: A voluntary pledge to fulfill an agreement.

Let's examine that definition again: **A voluntary pledge to fulfill an agreement.** Did you hear that? A vow is <u>a voluntary pledge</u>--not a <u>forced one.</u>

To fulfill an agreement--not as long as everything is going both parties' way; (or as long as the man treats you good, ladies). This is not what this definition is saying. There are no **ifs** or **buts** in this vow connected with the marriage statement a woman and man make at the wedding altar.

This is what the bible says concerning a vow: *"When thou shalt vow a vow unto the LORD thy God, thou shalt not slack to pay it: for the LORD thy God will surely require it of thee, and it would be sin in thee. But if thou shalt forbear to vow, it shall be no sin in thee. That which is gone out of thy lips thou shalt keep and perform..."* **(Deuteronomy 23:21-23a). KJV**

The above verses let us know that one can forbear to vow (a person does not have to make a vow), but if one makes a vow, they must perform it *(see it through)* **Vows**

are voluntary. Making a vow is left to the choice of a man or woman.

But once a vow is made, it is binding.

Ecclesiastes 5:4-5 teaches: "When you make a vow to God, do not delay to do it; for He has no pleasure in fools. Pay what you have vowed. It is **better not** to vow **than** to vow and not pay." (Forgive me, Lord, for being a fool over and over again).

Many *so-called* believers will stand before God and hear the words "depart from me,' because of the non-serious and careless vows they have made before God and man at the marriage altar.

I wish I had known earlier in life the thing about marriage and God's Word that I know now. If I had received the revelation about marriage that I have now, I wouldn't have had all of those failed marriages or made so many foolish choices.

I have always been the type of person *who believed if you make your bed hard, you should lie in it*. And for so many years, this is what I had done.

True repentance is being *Godly sorry* for one's sins and for the ungodly things one has done before a loving and gracious God whose eyes are in every place beholding the *good* and the *evil*.

I know now, without a doubt, that marriage for me would have been different if I had known then what I know now. Like many of you reading this book, I had never really looked at the marriage in such a severe manner or beheld this sacred union; through the eyes and **Word** of our Holy God. I would carelessly and casually enter into matrimony. And I would, at the first sign of trouble, *in a heartbeat*, **exit it.**

I wanted my marriage with Jerry, though. I wanted it to last. No one knows how much, but God does. I endured Jerry's mental abuse for over four years. When Jerry would knock me down--*by the force of his neglect and mental abuse*; just like a champion, I would get back up and continue in the fight.

In my shame and embarrassment and my efforts to save my marriage, I would get back up to get knocked down again and again by my husband's mental abuse and neglect.

Jerry would treat me good for a while, but he would start neglecting and abusing me again like that (a pop of the finger). For four years, I stayed in the ring, hoping that both Jerry and I could emerge victorious in the fight. But in the battle for our marriage, Jerry kept pushing me away; and pulling himself further and further away from me as he eased into the arms of another woman.

His words to me kept getting harsher and harsher. Now seeing my marriage through the eyes of God, the thing I should have done was to turn to God and allow **HIM** to be my main man and head until He dealt personally with Jerry.

I might have never looked at the marriage in this way if I hadn't come into that small church in Atlanta, Georgia, but now, I must forget my past failures and bravely move on.

The time started for the treatment of my wounds. When I had to remove the bandages and show the doctors my emaciated and wounded flesh, I felled-apart and wept bitterly. The medical team assured me that they understood my pain and told me to feel free just to let my emotions, feelings, and tears flow....***to just let it out***.

I never will forget the words that the wound doctor told me: *Mrs. Swims, I have no idea what it is like to see yourself this way, but I promise you I will do everything in my power to help you. Then there is always God—He will do all the things we just don't know how to do.*

Then I looked up at him. And just behind him, I saw a sign on the wall that assured me he meant what he said.

The sign read:

...for I know the thoughts that I have toward you, says the Lord, thoughts of peace and not of evil, to give you a future and a hope. **(Jeremiah 29:11)**

I cried even harder after reading this. Here was the Lord speaking to me through a sign posted on the center of this doctor's wall telling me that His plans were to give me a **future—and hope** for my life. People were touching my fragile body and assuring me that God would be right there with me **every step** of the way.

According to the plan my wound care doctor had made, I would go through 40 different treatments with hyperbaric. After that, they would attach a wound vacuum to my body until all the holes disappeared.

After informing me of this, my doctor looked at me and asked if I had any questions. I told him no. He then said, "I know it looks bad, and it is, but I have worked with much worst wounds than yours."

I told him that I trusted him, and the treatment was set up to start the preceding Monday. My son wasn't going to take me to every treatment because the center was so far from where we lived. But God had a ram in the bush. One of the church sisters volunteered to help me out when my son couldn't do it.

I wasn't able to drive during those first few weeks of the treatment, but I was praying to God every day to not tie up anyone's life and time dealing with me. I knew and believed that the woman from the church, who had volunteered to help me, didn't mind helping out.

I went to my wound treatments every day of the week. It was 40 minutes to an hour drive, depending on the traffic. After two weeks of my son and her dropping me off and picking me up, I cried out unto God and asked Him for help. The Holy Spirit told me to simply rest and trust him.... I was now able to drive.

I was still going to church on Sundays. Right after church, I would get back in bed and sleep until an hour and a half before my appointment. Then I would drive myself into Atlanta; get my treatment and drive back home and get back in bed. I was only getting out of the bed to shower, change my bandages and eat. I kept up this routine for the rest of time of my hyperbaric treatments. It was easier driving back because all I did during my treatment was lie in the hyperbaric chamber and watch television <u>*and/or*</u> a movie and relax.

Once I went into the chamber, they could not open it back up until my treatment time was over.

The time I stayed in the chamber always depended on the type of wounds I had and how bad the wounds were. They had explained that my time in the chamber would be the same as me being 350 feet below sea level. Due to that factor, they could not immediately take me out once my time in the chamber was over, but they had to slowly bring me out until my body was at back at its normal pressure.

I experienced bad days and good days during those 40 wound care treatments. After I would drive home from my treatment section, many times I would have to rest before I could get out of the car. Sometimes, I cried all the way back home. I felt lonely at times and wanted to give up.

This sister, who had been helping my son with me, would always know just when to call. She would bring me flowers, cards, and her husband would bless me with a few dollars every now and then. They had a lovely little girl and a very talented and handsome young son. This couple was like family to me and I claimed them as my own. I was very grateful to have them in my life.

God would always demonstrate his love and care for me...even beyond what I could think or ask. And now, he was using this family to display it. I was thankful for the **grace** (unmerited favor) and **mercy** he was lavishing upon me.

My big brother in the Lord would lift up my spirit, by talking to me about the goodness of the Lord and about the great things God was doing in our lives.

Finally, I was done with the hyperbaric treatments for my wounds...I had graduated. I received my certificate of completion, along with a picture of me with all the staff. A **Certified Hyperbaric Graduate**; *how about that?*

God was taking me from one level to another even though I didn't understand it. But I surely didn't want to go through what I was going through, to get to the place where God was taking me. What I went through though, was only drawing me closer to the LORD and to His will for my life.

It was now time for the next step in my treatments. I would now have to go through the wound vacuum treatment. The first time the wound vacuum wrap was put on me, it took the whole staff to figure out how to put it on me, because the wound was located on my chest. If the seal came loose at any point while they were trying to attach it to me, the procedure to apply the wrap would have to start over again...This almost drove me crazy, because it was always *coming loose* from my body. The embarrassment I endured by wearing this thing was unbelievable.

It was embarrassing to walk around with this tube dangling from underneath my clothes. Every child I came in contact with and even some adults would stare at me, when they would see the bloody fluids flowing through the tube.

I would be in church and as the pastor would start to preach, you could hear this gurgling sound coming from me, as the machine sucked the fluids from the wound. If this wasn't enough, an alarm would routinely go off, filling the sanctuary with the sound. And everyone would then turn and look at me and ask: "What is that?" I got tired of answering that question…I hated that vacuuming contraption.

The vacuum treatment finally ended. It had been an awful experience but the treatment had done its job. The holes in my chest had disappeared. Now, since my wounds were healed, it was time to go back to the surgeon so he could fill the hole left in my chest with a skin draft.

The day of my seventh surgery was sat. The surgeons would be reducing my left breast and using the material to fill in the hole on my right breast; rather than taking the skin from my leg like it was usually done…I came through this step with no problem. **All thanks be to God!**

All of my life I had considered my breasts to be too big and I wanted one day to get a breasts reduction. Who would have known that it would take me losing one of my breasts to get the chest reduction I wanted. I finally was smaller in the chest. **Thank you Jesus!**

I still had a long way to go concerning the physical problems on my right side, but I was ready to boldly face whatever I had to deal with.

God had been miraculously moving in my son's life also. He had met a beautiful young lady and they were engaged to be married. I knew this day would come and I was happy for them. The only thing I prayed was, *Lord, let her be good to my grandchildren. Let her love my grandchildren as though they were her own.*

I had known women who would date a man, pretending to love his children, but really did not. After they would marry the man, the children whom they pretended to adore and had treated like gold, they now barely tolerated.

Since the couple has married, I am very proud of my new daughter-in-law and of how she treats the kids. It was hard at first for me to hold my tongue when she would discipline them, but I didn't get in the way. I am now, thoroughly convinced, that she's a good mother to them.

With my son's new relationship came new plans, which included relocation. I was glad of this because I would once again have a place of my own.

God had led me to another Church by now. But through the ministry that I had previously attended, I had finally understood how to be a wife. My first husband was my Lord and Savior Jesus Christ, and I was *totally surrendered* and my heart was completed devoted to him.

I was now behaving like a married woman should. I was still married to Jerry, but my behavior didn't have anything to do with Jerry, but I had my eyes on God; as watery as they were with tears. And I would trust and follow Him and would not make a move until he instructed me.

Though the surgery was successful, I was suffering a lot of pain.

The Christmas season was coming back around and I was still not able to do much; except go to church and come back home.

Jerry, even being physically absent from my life, had occasionally been calling me with excuses. At least seven months had passed but he still would not make any move to stop holding up the divorce papers. It was plain to see that neither he nor his woman cared one way or the other about him divorcing me. But I cared. I was waiting on God to give me the direction of His will for Jerry and me.

The Christmas holiday had arrived, and my son and his children would all be out of town. That meant I would be home alone for the holidays.

My son had talked about sending me out of town to my baby brother's house; they would be out of town during the time. I wasn't physically able to make a trip, so I refused the offer.

While my family was gone, I cried and prayed the entire week before the Lord, seeking guidance for what I should do regarding my marriage with Jerry. I was sad and very depressed during the holidays, being there alone. Both day and night, I cried out unto God for answers. Please, God, show me what to do. *My husband is living his life as though I am already dead. Please, Please God, deliver me.*

Seven days in a row, I laid before the Lord, asking Him to move on my behalf. Whatever you do, Lord, I'm okay whether you bring him back or send him on. I will obey your decision.

That Sunday was New Year's Day, and my son and his family would be coming home the next day. I prayed this: One more year, God, and I am still alone without my husband. Nevertheless, I continued, **I can do all things, Lord because you strengthened me. (See Philippians 4:13).**

The very next morning, I was awakened by a phone call. It was Jerry. "I am on my way to see your lawyer and sign the papers for the divorce." He said. Then he continued, "I have decided that I don't want to give you any financial support." I didn't say a word. "Did you hear me, Joann?" he asked. Yes, I answered, *I hear you.* Then I hung up the phone.

The Lord had finally answered my prayer. As the head, Jerry had made his move. And the Lord was now losing me from my marriage with Jerry.

"*And a woman who has a husband, who does not believe, if he is willing to live with her, let her not divorce him...But if the unbeliever departs, let him depart; a brother or a sister is not under bondage in such cases, But God has called us to peace.*" **(I Corinthians 76:13, 15)**

I had been married to Jerry for almost four years before I was forced to let the marriage go. On June 6, 2011, I walked out of the courtroom in tears, but it was done. I was divorced from Jerry. I lost a lot by hooking up with that man. If I had had the strength, I would have believed God for a lawyer who could have fought for more of my financial rights.

I'm still paying for many things which I would not allow God to handle or control in my life. But through all the things I've been through and am still going through today, I am no longer **out of order.** God has freed me from my youth's pains and has broken the generational curses on my life and upon my family's. Any sexual bondage or spirit no longer enslaves me. I am now totally controlled by the **Holy Ghost**.

My focus now is totally upon the Word of God; therefore, I will no longer hold my peace and allow myself to be carried away with any wind or false doctrine. I am a believer, satisfied and Holy Ghost filled, living only for the Lord. I now face my trials and my fears with the assurance that Jesus will never leave me or forsake me.

I have had to have three more surgeries since I've written this book, and there are a few more up the road. But I am so thankful to God for how HE used this journey with all of the side effects and surgeries to bring me to *a place where I depend on HIM.* I was a messed-up person with little to no hope... but now I thank God and my Lord Jesus Christ!!! **I am healed from all my diseases!!!**

Thank you, Lord, for Cancer...For allowing it to come, and then for rebuking and causing it to go!

My journey is not over yet, but I have learned to trust and depend solely on God and His word through my ordeal. My trust and faith will always be grounded on the scripture I saw on the wall in the wound doctor's office **Jeremiah 29:11.**

The **King James Version of Jeremiah 29: 11** reads: "For I know the thoughts that I think toward you, saith the LORD, thoughts of peace, and not of evil, to give you an expected end." The **NRSV** version of this verse reads, "For surely I know the plans I have for you, says the LORD, plans for your welfare and not for harm, to give you a **future with hope."**

God has a *future with hope* for me, and that is why I can **THANK GOD FOR CANCER** while believing and knowing that: "...All things work together for the good of them who **love God**, to them who **are called** according to his purpose." **(Romans 8:28)**

I would now like to thank my readers for purchasing and reading my story. *But being Joann,* I must leave you with a **Word from God** and with a few nuggets of **TRUTH**. I know that many of you, like me, are going through struggles; or have suffered **sickness, heartaches, lack, loss**, and **wounds** from the fiery dots of the Enemy.

Therefore, I will end this book and leave you with the following instructions and words of exhortation.

"*Rejoice in the Lord always: and again, I say, Rejoice...Be careful for nothing; but in everything by prayer and supplication with thanksgiving let your requests be made known unto God. And the peace of God, which passeth all understanding, shall keep your hearts and minds through Christ Jesus.*" **(Philippians 4:4, 6-7)** The above words of God tell us always to rejoice, even when we're going through trials and struggles. Like Joseph, we must trust God even in our **Pits** of life. *We should be careful for nothing* (not worry about anything). But with thanksgiving, we should take our problems, pains, and struggles to God and leave them there with our **High Priest**. Our **Intercessor** is touched (moved) by the feelings of our infirmities, for *HE was wounded for our transgressions and bruised for our iniquities, and with his stripes we were healed.*

I Thessalonians, chapter 5 and verse 18 tells us this: "*In all things give thanks: for this is the will of God in Christ Jesus concerning you.*"

FINAL ACKNOWLEDGEMENTS

I would also like to thank Evangelist Lula McKinney-Walls, who brought Sister Tammara Denise Shepherd to our 2012 prayer conference. I acknowledge and thank Sister Shepherd for putting me in touch with her husband, Robert L. Shepherd Jr., the man who originally edited and published this book. *I strongly feel that Brother Shepherd was appointed by God Himself to edit my text.*

I would also like to thank and acknowledge all who read this book. **God bless you richly is my prayer!**

Pastor Joann Brown

My heartstrings

I want all my heartstrings to know "it's never too late to do something that they want to do in life!" My love for them will never die!!!

www.ingramcontent.com/pod-product-compliance
Lightning Source LLC
LaVergne TN
LVHW040135080526
838202LV00042B/2918